ND'S NOT JEWISH—HOW CAN HE PARTICIPATE IN THE CEREMONY? DO Y
BE OVER? WHEN DOES THE REAL MEAL BEGIN
ND SO IS MY MOTHER-IN-LAW! I DON'T KEEP KOSHER. DO
D WITH MATZO. MY HUSBAND'S NOT JEWISH—HOW CAN HE PARTICIPA
WHEN IS THIS SERVICE GONNA BE OVER? WHEN DOES THE REAL ME
SEDER! MY MOTHER IS COMING AND SO IS MY MOTHER-IN-LAW! I DON
I'M JEWISH, BUT I'VE NEVER COOKED WITH MATZO. MY HUSBAND'S N
VE TO DRINK FOUR GLASSES OF WINE? WHEN IS THIS SERVICE GONNA
'S MY TURN TO MAKE THE PASSOVER SEDER! MY MOTHER IS COMING A
KOSHER? WHO SELLS HAGGADAHS? I'M JEWISH, BUT I'VE NEVER COOK
E CEREMONY? DO YOU REALLY HAVE TO DRINK FOUR GLASSES OF WIN
WHERE DO I BEGIN? OH NO! IT'S MY TURN TO MAKE THE PASSOVER SED
ER. DOES A SEDER HAVE TO BE KOSHER? WHO SELLS HAGGADAHS?
HOW CAN HE PARTICIPATE IN THE CEREMONY? DO YOU REALLY HAVE
HEN DOES THE REAL MEAL BEGIN? WHERE DO I BEGIN? OH NO! IT'S
OTHER-IN-LAW! I DON'T KEEP KOSHER. DOES A SEDER HAVE TO BE KOSHE
MY HUSBAND'S NOT JEWISH—HOW CAN HE PARTICIPATE IN THE CEREM
S SERVICE GONNA BE OVER? WHEN DOES THE REAL MEAL BEGIN? WHE
THER IS COMING AND SO IS MY MOTHER-IN-LAW! I DON'T KEEP KOSH
UT I'VE NEVER COOKED WITH MATZO. MY HUSBAND'S NOT JEWISH—HO
OUR GLASSES OF WINE? WHEN IS THIS SERVICE GONNA BE OVER? WH
MAKE THE PASSOVER SEDER! MY MOTHER IS COMING AND SO IS MY MOT
O SELLS HAGGADAHS? I'M JEWISH, BUT I'VE NEVER COOKED WITH MATZ
O YOU REALLY HAVE TO DRINK FOUR GLASSES OF WINE? WHEN IS THIS SE
N? OH NO! IT'S MY TURN TO MAKE THE PASSOVER SEDER! MY MOTH
ER HAVE TO BE KOSHER? WHO SELLS HAGGADAHS? I'M JEWISH, BUT I'
ICIPATE IN THE CEREMONY? DO YOU REALLY HAVE TO DRINK FOUR GLA
MEAL BEGIN? WHERE DO I BEGIN? OH NO! IT'S MY TURN TO MAKE T
I DON'T KEEP KOSHER. DOES A SEDER HAVE TO BE KOSHER? WHO SE
ND'S NOT JEWISH—HOW CAN HE PARTICIPATE IN THE CEREMONY? DO Y
BE OVER? WHEN DOES THE REAL MEAL BEGIN? WHERE DO I BEGIN?
ND SO IS MY MOTHER-IN-LAW! I DON'T KEEP KOSHER. DOES A SEDER HA
D WITH MATZO. MY HUSBAND'S NOT JEWISH—HOW CAN HE PARTICIPA
WHEN IS THIS SERVICE GONNA BE OVER? WHEN DOES THE REAL

LET MY PEOPLE EAT!

The Festival of Passover is known as the

"Season of Our Freedom."

On the seasonal plane,

it marks the release of the earth from the grip of winter.

On the historical plane,

it commemorates the exodus of the Children of Israel from Egypt.

On the broad human plane,

it celebrates the emergence from bondage and idolatry.

—Theodor H. Gaster,
Festivals of the Jewish New Year

LET MY PEOPLE EAT!
PASSOVER SEDERS MADE SIMPLE

ZELL SCHULMAN

Macmillan • USA

MACMILLAN

A Simon & Schuster Macmillan Company
1633 Broadway
New York, NY 10019-6785

Macmillan Publishing books may be
purchased for business or sales promotional use.
For information please write:

Special Markets Department
Macmillan Publishing USA
1633 Broadway
New York, NY 10019

Library of Congress
Cataloging-in-Publication Data

Schulman, Zell. J., 1928–
    Let my people eat! : Passover seders made
simple / Zell Schulman.
        p.   cm.
    Includes bibliographical references and
index.
    ISBN 0-02-861259-0 (alk. paper)
    1. Passover cookery. I. Title.
    TX732.2.P37S38   1998   97-38973
    641.5'676437—dc21   CIP

Manufactured in the United States of America

        10 9 8 7 6 5 4 3 2
Book design and illustrations by Jennifer Abadi

DEDICATION

To

my dear husband and friend,

Mel Schulman,

and

in memory of my father,

Harry Sharff,

whose love of life and cooking inspired me, and who advised me to

"stay home from the movie and never budget on the stomach.

Always buy the best food."

TABLE OF CONTENTS

FOREWORD

Though I am not a wagering man, I would bet that most Jews, if asked their favorite Jewish holiday, would immediately answer: "Passover, *Pesach!*" Then, if asked why, they would certainly answer, "Because of the Seder!"

The Seder! It is a unique creation of the Jewish people. Sitting at the table with family, friends, and guests, we relive the story of our deliverance from bondage in Egypt. There are songs, discussions, questions, the rich pattern of observances. There is humor and fun, too. Some jokes are repeated year after year as if they were part of the ritual. There are even games at the Seder. Every year we live out and seek out the significance of the Divine call to move away from servitude to Pharaoh and all "gods" and toward the service of the one God of justice and mercy. It is a grand, moving experience, and at the same time, a very happy experience and lots of fun.

And, in answer to why it is so enjoyable a Jewish holiday, who would omit speaking of the Passover feast, the food, the special Passover dishes.

Because of this, many non-Jews love to be guests at a Passover Seder. There are interfaith Seders, and many non-Jewish groups want to put together something like a Seder for themselves.

So it is no surprise that the most published of Jewish books, in more editions than any other, is the Passover Haggadah, the table service, the narrative-ritual of the Passover Seder.

In like manner, there are many guides to the observance of Passover and to the preparation of the Seder feast.

But there is no guide to the Seder preparation as clear or effective as Zell Schulman's *Let My People Eat!* For both those who are endeavoring to have a Seder for the first time, and those who have had many years of experience preparing a Seder, this book is a real find.

Further, Zell Schulman's Seder guide and cookbook comes at the right time. The fact that family gatherings and bonding are ever more important to more and more of us is a prime reason that Passover is such a favorite among Jewish people. At the same time, numbers of people are ready and eager to go beyond a routine get-together using the old traditional Seder customs or foods. Many want to deepen the experience religiously while also giving all aspects of the Seder (including the food) additional taste and character. Coinciding with the importance of cherished intergenerational gatherings is the surge of interest in recovering our Jewish spirituality. But this is all happening at a time when many parents, including single parents, are working, and grandparents as well. People's lives are hectic and demanding.

So here is the book that provides the step-by-step guide to the preparation of a fine Seder feast; hands-on, immediate guidance as to how to get it done efficiently, without fuss, muss, or bother; where to go; what to get; and how to do it simply and directly. With this book one can avoid wasting precious time, whether in shopping or looking for explanations. It is all here, from A to Z, in one volume.

The book is great not only for first-timers (the author assumes no prior knowledge on the part of her readers), but also for those who have heretofore labored rigorously and sometimes tediously to get the Seder prepared.

At the same time, none of the reverence for the spiritual dimension of the Seder is lost. It is a book, in fact, meant to create a golden treasure trove of memories for generation after generation. Through it we are helped to continue the march of our people, led by a pillar of cloud by day and a pillar of fire by night, as the rabbis say, from degradation to glory.

So I say *Kol Ha Kavod*—high praise indeed—to Zell Schulman for her book, *Let My People Eat!* It will be a great boon to many.

RABBI HERBERT BRONSTEIN

—Chief Rabbi of North Shore Congegation Israel, Glencoe, Illinois and author of a best-selling Haggadah

ACKNOWLEDGMENTS

The road to publication has been an adventure. So many people all along the way have guided me, supported me, and participated with me in this creative endeavor. First and foremost, Jane Dystel, my literary agent, who believed in my idea, encouraged me to write a proposal, and introduced me to Lynn Stallworth, who edited it. Kirk Polking, my close friend and mentor, was always there to answer my questions and point me in the right direction. Pat Beusterien checked my manuscript and kept me on target. Her quiet and enthusiastic manner balanced my high-energy approach. Dorothy Larsson, R.D. and Julie Shapiro, R.D. spent many hours with me, checking and rechecking the recipes in the manuscript. My friends Dr. Richard S. Sarason and Dr. Sam Greengus, both on the faculty of Hebrew Union College Jewish Institute of Religion, Cincinnati Campus, were always ready with answers to my biblical questions and suggestions for biblical quotes. And I especially owe a big thank-you to my son Alan, a most talented and creative marketer, writer, and musician, who is responsible for the title: *Let My People Eat!: Passover Seders Made Simple.*

I wanted input from those who would use this book, so I created a focus group. I was thrilled when six outstanding cooks, Jewish and non-Jewish, volunteered. Eileen Chalfie, Janice Miller, Ilene Ross, Stacy Roth, and Judy Simon came together at every phase of development, giving me suggestions and ideas, as well as testing many of the recipes. I also wish to thank the many friends and relatives who tested recipes for me, giving the payment they received to their favorite charity.

Without the wonderful people at Macmillan Publishing, *Let My People Eat!* wouldn't be on the bookshelves. I was first introduced to Justin Schwartz of the cookbook division, who initiated me into this creative world of publishing. Then, my editor Amy Gordon took over, and she has been fabulous to work with. I learned a great deal from her, especially patience. She was always there for me, ready to listen and advise me. Thanks also to Jennifer Griffin, Senior Editor, Margaret Durante, Publicity Director, Wendy Coles in Special Sales, Tracy Crinion, Associate Marketing Manager, and Melissa Moyal, Production Editor. Sharing and learning about the various aspects of *Let My People Eat!* was a gift from each of them.

Last but not least, my most important critics and tasters, my children, who put up with all the frustrating times, especially when the computer and I weren't on the same wavelength: Stuart and Carol Ann, Karen and Avi, Alan and Linda, and Glenn and Carole.

INTRODUCTION

With two of my four children intermarried, a week or two before Passover my phone begins ringing off the hook. "What do I need besides the Seder plate?" "Where can I buy Haggadahs for the children?" "How many bottles of wine do I need? Do they have to be kosher for Passover?"

Let My People Eat! will answer all of your questions, teach you everything you've ever wanted to know about Passover, provide you with delicious and varied recipes, and put your mind at ease so you and your loved ones can enjoy this holiday.

Passover has always been my favorite holiday. Though raised in an Orthodox Jewish home, I've expanded my horizons. As a Reform Jew with an Orthodox heart, a Conservative way of life, and a husband and sons affiliated with a humanistic Jewish congregation, I've developed a new and broader acceptance of how others understand and celebrate this holiday. I look forward to sharing my varied Passover experiences and knowledge with family, friends, and students.

My mother and grandmother, of blessed memory, guided me from a very young age as we prepared the Seder. Over the years I watched and learned each step, from arranging the ceremonial Seder plate to preparing the traditional Passover Seder meal.

I remember how special I felt when I graduated from asking the four questions to opening the door for the prophet Elijah. And I'll never forget how my father, of blessed memory, always ended the Seder singing "God Bless America." He had come to America from Russia as a young man. He had a beautiful voice and was the cantor at our synagogue in Covington, Kentucky. Every year our family Seder ends with this song. The memory of his leading the Seder always makes Passover special for me.

While raising my children, I wrote, taught, and enlarged my understanding of the Jewish holidays, especially Passover. The Seder, with all its beauty and history, is the celebration I most enjoy.

I hope my step-by step approach to planning a Seder will be welcomed by anyone who wishes to celebrate Passover, including "first-timers," single parents, students far away from home, interfaith couples, and those who have been discouraged before. I've tried to make *Let My People Eat!* a guide as well as a cookbook, helping you through the duties and privileges of this most important celebration.

Although all recipes in *Let My People Eat!* will conform to the rules of kosher preparation for Passover, if so desired, you need not keep a kosher home to prepare your Seder from this book.

One of my primary concerns is addressing the needs of young adults whose family core is dispersed. They haven't the luxury of a grandmother or mother who can help them establish the Passover Seder celebration and rituals.

More and more Christian congregations, in true ecumenical spirit, honor the meaning of Passover by preparing model Seders. Why? Because the Passover message of the Jews' flight from slavery into freedom is a dramatic, exciting story, one that offers hope and promise of renewal to all people. The Passover Seder also provides the means of fulfilling our responsibility to engage and instruct the young. Best of all, it's a holiday filled with fun, entertainment, and wonderful food!

- Passover always occurs on the fifteenth day of Nisan (KNEE-sun), the first month in the Hebrew calendar, which coincides with late March or early April in the secular calendar. Passover is the first Jewish holiday mentioned in the Bible and has been observed by the Jewish people for more than three thousand years.

- The Israelites' hasty departure from Egypt, where they were slaves, as well as the explanation of the unleavened dough, which didn't have proper time to rise because the Israelites had to flee, is related in the Torah (TORE-ah): Exodus 12:17–19 and Exodus 13:8. Later, in Exodus 23:15, we read, "The feast of unleavened bread shall you keep; seven days you shall eat unleavened bread, as I commanded you . . . for . . . you came out of Egypt."

- The term Passover refers to the tenth plague, or that of the slaying of the first-born, in which the lamb's blood on the doorposts signaled the angel of death to "pass over" or "skip" the homes of the Israelites. The Hebrew *Pesach* (PAY-sahk) does not directly refer to the passing over but to the use of the lamb.

- Passover is referred to by two names in the Bible: *Chag Ha-Matzot* (HA-gah MA-tsot), the Feast of Unleavened Bread, and *Chag Ha-Pesach* (HA-gah PAY-sahk), referring to the Pesach, or "paschal," offering of a lamb or calf.

- The first name has various agricultural origins. In ancient Israel during this time of year, the spring crop of barley was ready for harvest, and one theory is that an offering of newly cut grain was made in thanks for the harvest. Grain from the previous year's harvest was to be cleaned out in preparation for the new crop; this may relate to the practice of removing leavened bread from the house.

- The second name is believed to refer to the offering of a lamb, which was an offering of thanks from the shepherd's flock, similar to the grain offering in biblical times. During Passover, Jews are prohibited from eating or possessing any foods that have come in contact with leavened foods or could become subject to a leavening process. These foods are called *Chometz* (Haw-METZ), meaning leavened or fermented. Those following Ashkenazic Passover traditions do not eat or prepare foods made with grains such as wheat, rye, oats, barley, or corn. These grains are similar to those that are used to bake bread and are prohibited for Passover.

- Matzo (MOTT-seh) has endured for more than 5,000 years. Baked without leavening, it is the only type of bread eaten during Passover. When the Israelites were told to be prepared to leave quickly, they had no time to allow their bread to rise, so the dough was baked immediately in the form of round, flat cakes or crackers. Matzo can be made from any of a number of grains, although wheat is currently the most commonly used. It can be round or square. Machine-made matzo is typically square.

- Seder (SAY-der) means "order." Held in the home, the Seder begins after sundown the evening before the first day of the Passover holiday. For generations, the arrangement of the Seder table and Seder plate, the Seder meal, the readings, the songs, and the eating of symbolic foods have followed a certain "order."

- The Seder is divided into four parts: welcoming in the holiday with the traditional candle lighting, blessings over the first cup of wine, partaking of the green vegetable, and breaking of the middle matzo; retelling the story of the Exodus and partaking of the ceremonial foods; eating the Seder festive meal; and finally, reciting prayers of thankfulness, welcoming Elijah the prophet, and singing Passover songs.

A special book called a Haggadah (Ha-GOD-ah), meaning "to tell" or "relate," is used at the Passover Seder. Dating from the first century of the Common Era, it provides the order in which the story of the Exodus is told. The Haggadah also explains the Passover symbols and contains liturgical text, prayers, and songs.

The number four appears often in the Haggadah: the four cups of wine, the four questions, the four sons. In ancient times the number four was thought to have some magical or mystical significance. Others say it relates to God's four promises made to the Israelites when they were freed from Egypt.

I will bring you out of the land of bondage.

I will save you.

I will free you from slavery.

I will take you to be a chosen people.

—Exodus 6:6–7

WHERE DO I BEGIN?

This year it's your turn to make the Passover Seder! Your mother may decide to come, and your mother-in-law is definitely coming. No need to panic. The word Seder means "order." So, figuratively put your hand in mine, and together we'll prepare the meaningful and significant ceremonial foods for the Seder plate and the festive meal and set a beautiful Seder table.

Nowhere is it written that you must, or need to, follow in your family's footsteps or keep kosher to have a Seder. Many "secular" Jews who do not celebrate other religious holidays or practices celebrate Passover with a Seder and festive meal in their homes. *Individuality* is the key word. Planning your Seder is like planning a party. Begin by asking yourself the following questions:

- Do I want to hold the Seder in my home, taking into account the amount of preparation this entails?

- Do I want to have just one Seder, or would I enjoy sharing the second night with friends and having two Seders?

- Do I want to consider asking friends or family to share in the Seder preparations with me?

- How many can I accommodate comfortably in my home?

- Do I want a traditional or modern Seder?

- Do I want to cook all or part of the menu?

- Will there be company coming from out of town?

- How many guests will wish to bring their children with them?

As for any special event, it's better to begin planning four to six weeks before the first Passover Seder. Since Passover is a spring holiday, you may wish to begin your spring cleaning. Traditionalists like my mother and grandmother removed all leavened foods, such as canned and dried legumes and other Chometz, from their kitchens. They also used separate dishes, flatware, and cooking utensils for Passover which had not come in contact with any leavened foods.

Those who, like me, tend to be a little more lenient with the Passover dietary laws, don't necessarily follow all the traditions. Beautiful disposable china, linens, and serving pieces are available today. These can be a real asset, especially if there are small children at the Seder.

Preparing for Passover should be an adventure rather than a chore. Consider trying some of these pre-Passover cleaning suggestions:

- Check the pantry, cupboard, or closet where you keep cereals or other items that may have leavening. Remove them and take them to an organization that feeds the homeless.

- Shelves may need wiping off or may need new coverings.

- Look over your appliances and ovens, making sure they are all clean and in working condition.

- Try having all home repairs or redecorating completed on time.

- Check your linens, china, glasses, flatware, serving pieces, and platters. Be sure you have what is needed for your Seder.

CHOOSING THE MENU

Passover is the culinary pinnacle of the Jewish year. It's also an enjoyable and memorable time for families and friends to get together. More and more, nondenominational "mock" Seders are being held. We read in the Bible that the holiday of Passover is celebrated for seven days. Many homes prepare one or two Seders and follow the traditions of their ancestors for the entire week. For others, preparing and participating in a Seder holds the most significance. I have created six distinct Seder menus to choose from.

ASHKENAZIC
(OSH-KEH-NOZ-ZEEK)

This Seder is the most familiar and popular. The menu contains the foods of those Yiddish-speaking Jews whose families migrated to America from northern and eastern European countries between 1880 and 1920.

SEPHARDIC
(SEH-FAR-DEEK)

The foods in this Seder are from the Jews from the Mediterranean countries. These were the Spanish and Portuguese Jews who fled from the Spanish Inquisition and went to Turkey, Greece, Italy, and Israel. North African Jewry also prepare foods in the Sephardic manner.

"OFF-THE-SHELF"

This Seder uses prepared or packaged foods certified "kosher for Passover," which you can enhance with a personal touch.

HEALTHFUL

This is a flavorful menu for those monitoring their fat and cholesterol intake.

VEGETARIAN

This Seder menu contains no fish, meat, or poultry, and offers creative vegetable entrées.

ECUMENICAL POTLUCK

For this Seder, Jewish and non-Jewish friends come together, each preparing and bringing a variety of foods.

The recipes chosen for these Seder menus are a blend of religious precept, custom, history, and gastronomy. You may wish to follow each Seder menu completely, or choose those recipes that appeal to you and develop your own menu.

Following each menu are the recipes, a shopping list of ingredients, and a preparation timetable that breaks down the work into several steps.

The ceremonial portion of the Seder is discussed in great detail in chapter 3. An explanation of the significance of the ceremonial foods on the Seder plate is followed by recipes for the Seder plate, a shopping list, and preparation timetable.

WHAT DO I NEED FOR MY SEDER AND WHERE CAN I BUY IT?

For Seven Days thereafter you shall eat unleavened bread . . . for you departed from the land of Egypt hurriedly—so that you may remember the day of your departure from the land of Egypt as long as you live.

—Deut. 16:3

STOCKING YOUR PANTRY FOR PASSOVER

According to Jewish dietary law, all kosher for Passover food product items must be labeled with the correct Passover kosher symbol. The word *kosher* (KO-sher) means "fitting." The symbol indicates that the ingredients, machinery, and facilities used by the manufacturer in the production of the commercially packaged products have been monitored under "strict orthodox supervision" by a rabbi or rabbinical student knowledgeable about the kosher laws.

PROHIBITED FOODS

The following general guide to food for Passover is adapted from the Passover guide of the Rabbinical Assembly Committee on Jewish Law and Standards, accepted on December 12, 1984.

- Breads, cakes, biscuits, crackers, cereals, and coffees containing leavening agents are forbidden.

- Wheat, barley, oats, corn, and rye are forbidden because they are grains similar to those that are used to bake bread.

- All beverages containing ingredients or flavors made from grain alcohol are forbidden because of the grain.

- For those of Ashkenazic persuasion, rice, corn, millet, and legumes such as beans and peas are forbidden. These all have kernels that swell or rise when cooked and are the grains used to bake bread.

- For those of Sephardic persuasion, rice and legumes have always been a part of the diet, often as a main source of protein, so these never became forbidden in Sephardic communities.

SHOPPING FOR YOUR SEDER

The word Seder literally means "order of the ritual." Passover, with all its history and symbolism, provides an opportunity for each person or family to create their own rituals. I look forward to opening the boxes of Passover ceremonial items that were packed away the previous year. After checking to make sure everything is in good order, I prepare a shopping list. Shopping for your Seder needn't be an ordeal. Checklists seem to ease the stress.

CHECKLIST OF CEREMONIAL ITEMS

Seder plate for the ceremonial foods

Container for salt water

Haggadah (Ha-GOD-dah) for each person

Pair of candlesticks

Two small, white holiday candles

Kiddush (KI-dish) cup for the leader

Smaller wineglasses for the guests

Matzo holder with pockets (optional)

Afikoman (OFF-ee-comb-man) bag (optional)

Wine goblet for Elijah the prophet

Decanter for wine

Yarmulkah (YAHR-m'l-keh) head covering (optional)

Pillow for reclining (optional)

SIGNIFICANCE OF THE CEREMONIAL ITEMS

SEDER PLATE

The Seder plate contains the symbolic foods needed for retelling the Passover story. It is set near the leader's place. If you don't wish to purchase a decorative Seder plate, use small custard cups or ramekins to hold the symbolic foods and set them on a decorative tray or platter.

CONTAINER FOR SALT WATER

A container is needed to hold the salt water into which the symbolic parsley, radish, or celery is dipped. This is to remind us of the tears and sweat the Jewish people shed when they were enslaved in Egypt.

HAGGADAHS

The Haggadah, which means "to tell," contains the story of the Exodus, the prayers, songs, rituals, and commentary. It's nice to have one at each place, but if you don't, sharing is okay. If there isn't room on the table, set them on the seat of each chair. The leader may also give them out after everyone is seated.

CANDLESTICKS WITH CANDLES

The lighting and blessing of the candles, done before the Seder begins, welcomes in the holiday and is symbolic of the joy of the celebration. Pure paraffin white holiday candles made in Israel are usually used, but long tapers of other colors are also appropriate. These are set before the person saying the blessing. Historically and traditionally, this has been done by a woman, young girl, or daughter of the family. Today it is not unusual to have a man, young boy, or son perform the ritual.

KIDDUSH CUP

A prayer called the kiddush is recited by the leader over a cup filled with wine. The sanctity of the Sabbath or festival is affirmed in this prayer. It is customary for this traditional goblet, called a kiddush cup, to be made of precious metal.

SMALL WINEGLASSES

An important part of the Seder ritual is consuming four cups of wine or grape juice. These are symbolic of the four things God promised his people (Exodus 6:6–7): "I will bring you out of the land of bondage." "I will save you." "I will free you from slavery." "I will take you to be a chosen people."

According to the Orthodox Union, you needn't consume more than three fluid ounces in each cup, so I purchase small wineglasses to use during the ceremonial part of the Seder.

MATZO HOLDER

Three special whole matzos play a significant role in telling the Passover story. These three matzos are placed in a special matzo holder or in a white napkin, folded over twice, with one matzo placed in between each fold (see illustration). The top and bottom matzos represent the two traditional loaves

set out in the ancient temple during all Jewish holidays. The middle matzo represents the Passover festival. According to modern interpretation, these three matzos also represent the three divisions of the Jewish people.

Kohen (KO-hayn): the priest of the temple

Levi (LEE-vie): assistants in the temple

Israelites: the people of Israel

AFIKOMAN BAG

The middle matzo, called the Afikoman, is of Greek origin but uncertain etymology, and has been interpreted as "dessert." After the destruction of the temple, it became a symbolic reminder of the paschal lamb and is the last ceremonial food eaten at the Seder. The leader hides half of the Afikoman in a special decorated bag or a napkin. The children search and redeem it in exchange for a present.

ELIJAH'S WINE GOBLET

A large, beautiful, decorative goblet filled with wine is placed in a prominent spot on the table to welcome Elijah the prophet, who is supposed to return to earth before the coming of the messiah and settle all disputes about Jewish law. According to the legend, Elijah visits each Passover Seder to herald freedom and redemption.

YARMULKAH

During the early Middle Ages, the rabbis decided man should cover his head as a sign of respect before God. Orthodox and Conservative Jews follow this custom. Today the yarmulkah (*kippah* in Hebrew) has become a recognizable symbol of the Jew. This custom is also common among other peoples of the East, from Arabia to India.

PILLOW FOR RECLINING

The leader is provided with a pillow to recline against during certain portions of the Seder service, symbolizing the comfort enjoyed by free men when dining.

SHOPPING FOR CEREMONIAL ITEMS

Ceremonial items for Passover come in a variety of prices, sizes, and styles. They can be found in temple gift shops, mail-order catalogs, on America Online (AOL), or the World Wide Web (look for sources specializing in or listed under Judaica). Orthodox, Conservative, and Reform houses of worship are all listed under "Synagogues" in the Yellow Pages. Ask to speak to someone in the gift shop.

HAGGADAHS

The Haggadah used at the Seder includes the story of the Exodus, prayers, songs, rituals, and commentary, all laid out in a significant order.

At the Passover Seder we are obligated to engage and instruct the young in retelling the story of the Exodus. The Haggadah allows us to fulfill this obligation.

Jews throughout the world have been using Haggadahs since the first century of the Common Era. For thousands of years, many readings, songs, and poems have been added to the Haggadah.

Different communities have printed their own Haggadahs, and there are many current options. More than 3,000 editions of the Haggadah are catalogued in the library of the Jewish Theological Seminary in New York, and every year more versions appear.

Before purchasing Haggadahs, you may wish to visit your local library or the library of your synagogue or temple to see what's available. Check out several Haggadahs that appeal to you. Haggadahs are also sold through mail-order catalogs and in many chain bookstores.

SUGGESTED CURRENT HAGGADAHS

A Passover Haggada, The New Union Haggadah, edited by Rabbi Herbert Bronstein, drawings by Leonard Baskin (New York: Central Conference of American Rabbis, 1982, $29.95).

Beautifully illustrated, this Haggadah takes a modern approach. Used by many Reform temples at their congregational Seders, the format in Hebrew and English with transliterations is easy to follow. The drawings stimulate discussion between grandchildren, parents, and grandparents.

The Passover Celebration, edited by Rabbi Leon Klenicki (Chicago: The Anti-Defamation League of B'Nai Brith and Liturgy Training Publications, Archdiocese of Chicago, 1985, $2.25). "Songs for the Seder Meal," a half-hour cassette ($5.95) is also available. Both may be ordered by calling 1-800-933-1800.

This Haggadah was prepared, with Jewish and Christian sponsorship, to help Christians learn about and celebrate a Seder that includes much of the richness of the Jewish liturgy. Its text is easily followed and its explanations of the history and rituals are easily understood. The tape contains music for the Seder meal. The pronunciation on the tape of the Hebrew songs and prayers used most often in the Seder is very clear.

The Crown Haggadah (Printed in Israel and distributed in America by Caspari Cards, $39.95).

This is a collector's dream. Max Frankel, Executive Director of the Bureau of Jewish Education in Cincinnati, told me, "The original edition was done on deerskin parchment and sells for one hundred thousand dollars." The artistry, design, and calligraphy are breathtaking. Written in Hebrew and English, the text, though scholarly and traditional, is beautifully presented.

A Family Haggadah, by Shoshana Silberman. Illustrated by Katherine Janus Kahn (Rockville, Maryland: Kar-Ben Publishers, 1996, $3.39).

A companion audiocassette is $10.95. The text is in Hebrew-English with transliterations and simple translations. This book has a visual key to guide you through it. A child's face designates activities for young children; a pencil alerts you to activities the family can do together or plan ahead; and a musical note denotes places where songs are to be sung. The cassette contains Seder blessings and songs cued to the Haggadah.

WORDS AND SYMBOLS ON FOODS FOR PASSOVER

Across the United States, more than 15 kosher symbols can be found on kosher products. A "K" may claim that the product is kosher but it doesn't have rabbinical supervision.

The following words or symbols are universally found on products that are kosher for Passover. These indicate that the product is certified for Passover with proper rabbinical supervision. When in doubt about a product or symbol, ask your rabbi.

D or milchig (MILK-heeg) signifies food that contains milk or milk products. Dairy foods must come from a kosher animal.

M or fleishig (FLAY-sheeg) designates the product is for meat use only.

Pareve (PA-rev) or parve (PAR-va) indicates products that contain neither meat, milk, nor their by-products. They are neutral and may be eaten with milk or meat.

"Kosher for Passover" or "kosher l'Pesach" (KO-sher-l'PAY-sahk) indicates just that, that the product is okay to eat during Passover.

SYMBOLS TO LOOK FOR

(U)P The symbol of the Union of Orthodox Jewish Congregations, New York

(U) with the words "Kosher for Passover"

(U) with the words "May be used for Passover"

(K)P The symbol of organized Kashrus Laboratories, New York

(Ɔ)P The symbol of Kof-K Kosher supervision, Teaneck, New Jersey

BUT IS IT KOSHER?

Kosher cooking today is the result of two distinct influences: first, the demands of Jewish law governing the preparation and presentation of food, and second, the customs of people among whom the Jews have lived for the last 3,000 years. For instance, there is a prohibition against mixing meat and dairy foods, which is based on the biblical injunction, "You shall not seethe a kid in its mother's milk."

The word *kosher* literally means "fit or proper" and describes those types of foods that Torah law declares fit to eat as well as the selection and preparation of foods that have been carried out in accordance with traditional Jewish ritual and dietary laws. Kosher foods include three classifications: meat, dairy, and pareve.

Because the wide variety of ingredients used in packaged foods makes it difficult to determine whether a product is kosher, the manufacturing of the product must be supervised by a rabbi. When this is the case, the package label includes the name of the rabbi or an identifying symbol, or both.

MEAT

Kosher meat must come from an animal that chews its cud and has split hooves. It must be slaughtered according to the dietary laws by a shochet (SHOW-keht), a ritual slaughterer of meat and fowl. The permissible parts of the animal must be salted before cooking. In the Bible there is an absolute prohibition against the consumption of blood (Leviticus 17:12), and thus blood must be extracted from the meat through salting or broiling.

Any food made with meat or fowl, or meat and fowl products such as bones, soup, or gravy, is considered fleishig, or "meat." Most kosher butchers "kosher" the meat for their customers—which means they soak the meat or poultry in salted water before selling it for cooking. As a rule, frozen meat sold by a kosher butcher is koshered.

DAIRY

Any food derived from milk is considered milchig. Dairy foods must come from a kosher animal, have no meat fats or any kind of meat substances mixed into them, and contain no non-kosher substances. Dairy foods must have Jewish supervision from the time of milking through their complete processing and have kosher verification on the label. They are sold in groceries and supermarkets across the country.

PAREVE (OR PARVE)

This term includes foods that are neither meat nor dairy. They may be cooked and eaten with meat or dairy. Pareve foods include fish, eggs, leafy vegetables, fruits, grains, and oil.

FISH

Fish must have both fins and scales and swim in oceans, seas, or rivers. Shellfish, such as shrimp, oysters, and crabs, lack fins and scales and are scavengers and therefore are not considered kosher.

KOSHER EGGS

Kosher eggs must come from kosher fowl. A blood spot in an egg, whether it's raw or cooked, renders the egg nonkosher.

PROCESSED VEGETABLES, FRUITS, AND GRAINS

Any processed vegetable, fruit, or grain that could contain worms and insects must be approved by a certified kosher inspector before it can be packaged and sold. These products have kosher verification on the labels.

OILS

While olive oil was used by Jews for centuries as the main cooking oil, northern and eastern European Jews had little access to it and depended instead on butter or meat fats for cooking. Since butter (dairy) cannot be eaten with meat, and since lard (a pork product) is forbidden to Jews, chicken and other poultry fats have always figured importantly in a number of cuisines evolving from these parts of Europe. Nowadays, in recipes where oil or shortening is required, only a pure vegetable shortening made under rabbinical supervision may be used. As with most pareve foods, these oils bear kosher verification on their labels and are sold in supermarkets and groceries.

During Passover, specific dietary laws are enforced and foods must be certified as kosher for Passover or kosher l'Pesach.

When shopping for kosher foods, always check for dairy, meat, and pareve status. Also check the labels for the marks of certification, keeping in mind that the symbols vary in different parts of the country. In some product lines, only certain flavors or varieties are kosher.

STAPLES FOR YOUR PASSOVER PANTRY

Each year more and more new "kosher for Passover" products are available in supermarkets and specialty stores. What was once a shopping chore has turned into a culinary adventure.

Matzo comes in many shapes, sizes, and flavors. You can get low-fat, no-fat, and yolk-free Passover foods. Sponge cake, for years the dessert of choice, now has competition. The variety of tortes, cookies, and cakes found on the shelves and in the freezer section is overwhelming. The dairy counters are overflowing. Buttermilk and whipping cream sit side-by-side with soft and hard cheeses like ricotta, cheddar, gouda, Parmesan, mozzarella, and Swiss. The Passover sauces and salad dressings available today will have entrées and salads taking center stage.

There are still basic Passover products, essential for the Passover pantry, especially matzo, a crisp, flat, unleavened bread made of flour and water, which must be baked in 18 minutes, before the dough has had time to rise. Matzo and the matzo products used in place of flour for cooking and baking are manufactured under rabbinical supervision specifically for Passover use, and must carry the proper Passover symbol. Matzo is the only type of "bread" that may be eaten during Passover by those Jews wishing to follow the dietary guidelines. Rabbinical authorities differ on what is permissible for Passover. It is always advisable to check with a rabbi.

PRODUCTS TRADITIONALLY USED FOR PASSOVER

Each year, new Passover products are available. If you're concerned about whether they're kosher for Passover, check with a rabbi. For mail-order gift and food catalogs, see page 198.

MATZO PRODUCTS

Whole matzos: plain, tea, egg, yolk-free, whole wheat

Farfel: broken pieces of matzos

Matzo meal: coarsely ground matzos

Matzo cake meal: finely ground matzos

BAKING PRODUCTS

Unopened jars and boxes that do not have additives (including salt or sugar), if purchased before Passover, can be used for cooking and require no Passover certification.

Potato starch (also used for thickening)

Vanilla sugar (available in packets; 1 or 2 teaspoons is equivalent to 1 teaspoon vanilla extract)

HERBS AND SPICES

There are many types of fresh herbs available in the produce department of your supermarkets and specialty stores. Unopened jars and boxes of herbs and spices that were purchased before Passover and that do not have additives may be used for cooking and require no Passover certification.

PRODUCTS TO AVOID

CONDIMENTS

Mustard seed grows in pods, so it is considered a legume; therefore, mustard cannot be used at Passover.

OILS

Corn oil is one of the prohibited foods because corn is one of those foods that is used for leavening.

CONFECTIONERS' SUGAR

Only confectioners' sugar made with potato starch, not cornstarch, is permissible during Passover. This product has limited distribution.

VANILLA EXTRACT

Regular vanilla extract contains grain alcohol. Kosher for Passover extract is prepared without an alcohol base; it is available but might be a little harder to find.

PREPARING THE SEDER PLATE AND SETTING THE SEDER TABLE

What is the meaning of this rite? You shall say: It is the Lord's Passover, for he passed over the houses of the Israelites in Egypt when God struck the Egyptians but spared our houses.

—Exodus 12:26–27

Interest in participating in a Seder continues to increase each year. More and more "mock" Seders are being held by many denominations. The major elements for the ceremonial portion of the Seder are described in great detail, along with illustrations, in this chapter.

CEREMONIAL FOODS ON THE SEDER PLATE

The Seder Plate—Kaarah (CAR-ah)

The Seder plate contains representative portions of the ceremonial foods, each one having a symbolic meaning. These ceremonial foods are listed in the order in which they're described in the Haggadah.

A. PARSLEY OR CELERY LEAVES—KARPAS (CAR-pass)

Symbolizes springtime, hope, and renewal.

SALT WATER

Represents the tears of slavery.

B. A ROASTED EGG— BAYTZAH (BAYTZ-ah)

Symbolizes the festival offering brought to the temple. It also represents the flowering of new life in the spring.

Vegans can substitute a beet, avocado pit, or potato for the egg.

C. ROASTED BONE— ZEROAH (ZAIR-oh-AH)

Represents the ancient sacrifice of the paschal lamb. Lamb was eaten by the Jewish people at the first Passover. Today many families use a roasted wing from a chicken.

Vegetarians/vegans can substitute a mushroom for the shank bone.

D. HORSERADISH OR ROMAINE LETTUCE—MAROR (MAR-or)

Symbolizes the bitterness our forefathers experienced in Egypt as slaves. Ashkenazim use the horseradish root; Sephardim use romaine lettuce.

E. APPLE OR DRIED FRUIT, NUT, AND WINE MIXTURE— CHAROSET (HA-row-SET)

Symbolizes the mortar our Jewish ancestors used to make bricks in building Pharaoh's cities.

I place a small container for the salt water in the center of my Seder plate and cut up small portions of parsley.

Suggested Wines for the Ceremonial Portion of the Seder

Kedem—Cream Red Concord

Kesser—Seven Seventy/Kiddush Wine

Kesser—Passover Eminent Dry

Setting The Seder Table

The Seder table represents the stage upon which the drama of the Israelites' exodus from Egypt is played out. The ceremonial objects, place settings, and festive dinner create the set. The person guiding you through the Haggadah plays the lead, and those participating are the cast. The total production is in your hands.

The diagram on the following page shows one way to set your Seder table. Using the place settings and ceremonial objects you've chosen, set the table in a manner most comfortable for you, your family, and your guests. Flowers are a nice addition but not necessary.

The following items are placed on the table:

Tablecloth and napkins

China, glassware, and flatware

Seder plate with the ceremonial foods

Container with salt water for dipping

Haggadahs for each person

Pair of candlesticks

Two small, white holiday candles

Kiddush cup for the person leading the Seder

Small wineglasses for the guests

Matzo holder with pockets (optional) or 3 matzos covered in a folded napkin

Afikoman bag (optional)

Wine goblet for Elijah the prophet

Decanter for wine (or bottle of wine)

Extra pitcher of salt water

Extra horseradish for Seder meal

Extra matzo for Seder meal

Extra charoset for Seder meal

Wine coaster (optional)

Flowers (optional)

Individual Seder plates with parsley, horseradish, and charoset (optional)

A. Haggadah

B. Grape Juice Decanter

C. Red Wine Decanter

D. Kiddish Cup

E. Matzo Holder

F. Extra Matzos for Seder Meal

G. Pair of Candlesticks

H. Elijah's Cup

I. Salt Water

PURPOSE OF EXTRA ITEMS ON THE TABLE

Decanter of Wine

A decanter or two of wine, plus one of grape juice for those who don't drink wine, is useful for refilling the glasses. For years, only sweet wine was kosher for Passover. Now an extensive selection of white, red, blush, and rosé wines, as well as liqueurs, are kosher for Passover.

Extra Matzos

There are special square Passover matzo platters available to hold the matzos, but a serving plate also works. As bread is prohibited at Passover, matzos are needed for both the service and the main meal.

Extra Charoset

Although there is charoset on the Seder plate, extra is needed for preparing Hillel's symbolic sandwich. In observance of the precept that says, "They shall eat it [the paschal lamb] together with matzo and bitter herbs," the scholar Hillel combined bitter herbs and charoset and ate them together on matzo.

Extra Horseradish

Although horseradish is on the Seder plate, another container is filled with horseradish for the participants to eat during dinner and for Hillel's sandwich. This horseradish may be freshly grated or purchased in a jar.

Extra Pitcher of Salt Water

In some homes it is the custom to begin the festive meal with a hard-boiled egg on which salt water is added instead of plain salt. A pitcher is an easy way to pass the salt water. I keep it in the refrigerator, then place it on the table just before the festive meal is about to begin.

Lamb Shank Bone or Chicken Wing

I can't always get a lamb shank bone, so sometimes I use a raw chicken wing. I prefer the broiling method, but I have also included a method for roasting. This can be done several days ahead, wrapped well in aluminum foil, and kept in the refrigerator until you are ready to prepare the Seder plate.

1 lamb shank bone, or 1 chicken wing

Broiling Method

Preheat the broiler to its highest setting. Place the shank bone or chicken wing on aluminum foil. Set it about 6 inches under the broiler. When broiled well on one side, about 2 minutes, turn it over and broil it well on the other side, 1 to 2 more minutes. Keep watch, as it can get black. Cool for 5 to 10 minutes before you refrigerate it.

Roasting Method

Preheat the oven to 325°F. Place the shank bone or chicken wing on aluminum foil. Allow it to roast for 45 to 50 minutes or until good and brown.

ASHKENAZIC ROASTED EGG

Until I was married, my grandmother always insisted I eat the roasted egg after the Seder. She believed it would bring me a husband. I respected her wishes and always consumed the egg. You can roast the egg in a toaster oven if you prefer. It can be prepared several days ahead, wrapped well, and refrigerated until you are ready to prepare the Seder plate.

1 large egg

1. Place the egg in a small saucepan. Cover it with cold water and bring to a boil. Reduce the heat and simmer, uncovered, for about 12 minutes. Remove the egg from the water.

2. Preheat the oven to 400°F. Place the egg on aluminum foil; roast for 20 to 30 minutes, turning it now and then, until the eggshell is brown and splits a little.

SEPHARDIC ROASTED EGG, OR HUEVOS HAMINADOS

These eggs are roasted overnight. They get a rich brown color and are served in their shells. They have a creamy, rich flavor. In the traditional method of cooking, tea leaves are added to the water and the eggs are simmered for 6 hours. The following method is simpler. One of the eggs may be used for the Seder plate, and the others served at the beginning of the festive meal. These can be prepared several days ahead, placed in a covered container, and refrigerated.

8 large eggs

Preheat the oven to 225°F. Place the eggs in a deep casserole. Pour boiling water over the eggs, about double the volume of the eggs. Cover tightly and bake for 8 hours or overnight. Drain and serve.

ASHKENAZIC CHAROSET

MAKES 2 CUPS

This is the recipe I use for my Passover Seder. It doubles easily. Prepare it the morning of the Seder, cover it well, and then refrigerate.

1 cup chopped nuts (pecans, almonds, walnuts, or a mixture)

5 small apples, peeled and cored

1 teaspoon grated lemon zest

3 tablespoons sweet wine, or more to taste

1½ tablespoons sugar

1 tablespoon ground cinnamon

1 teaspoon ground ginger

Processor Method

1. Place the nuts in the bowl of a food processor fitted with the metal blade. Pulse 2 to 3 times to chop. Remove to a small bowl and set aside.

2. Cut the apples into 1-inch pieces. Add to the food processor with the lemon zest, wine, sugar, cinnamon, and ginger. Pulse 2 to 3 times until everything is chopped into medium pieces. Scrape the bowl as needed, making sure nothing gets lodged on the blade. Remove to a 1-quart bowl. Fold in the nuts, adjust the seasonings, then cover and refrigerate.

Conventional Method

With a sharp knife, chop the nuts and dice the apples into a 1-quart bowl. Add the lemon zest, wine, sugar, cinnamon, and ginger and combine. Adjust the seasonings, then cover and refrigerate.

SEPHARDIC CHAROSET

MAKES APPROXIMATELY 3¹/₂ CUPS

This recipe looks more like a jam when you're finished. I find that soaking the dates and raisins in boiling water for 10 to 15 minutes and then draining them makes them easier to chop. Charoset can be prepared two or three days before the Seder, covered well, and refrigerated.

8 ounces pitted dates

4 ounces golden raisins

4 ounces dark raisins

1 Granny Smith apple

2 teaspoons sweet wine

¹/₄ cup orange juice

1 teaspoon ground ginger

¹/₂ cup blanched slivered almonds

1. Soak the dates and raisins in boiling water for 10 to 15 minutes. Core the apple, cut it into 2-inch pieces, and place in a 1-quart bowl. In a separate bowl, mix the wine, orange juice, and ginger together.

2. Place the drained dates and raisins and the apple in the bowl of a food processor fitted with the metal blade or in a blender. Pulse several times; add the nuts and the wine mixture. Pulse several times until you have a coarse paste. Empty into a bowl, cover well, and refrigerate.

HORSERADISH

MAKES APPROXIMATELY 3 CUPS

Both red and white horseradish can be purchased in a jar. However, I prefer a combination of fresh ground horseradish and horseradish from a jar for Passover. I cut off the root end of the horseradish and put it on my Seder plate. (I try choosing a root that has some green sprouting from its top.) I peel and grind a small portion of the rest of the horseradish root in my food processor, then add it to the horseradish from the jar. I use this for the Seder meal.

It's easy to make horseradish with a food processor or blender. I also place slices of horseradish in a small bowl on my Seder table for Hillel's sandwich. The horseradish can be prepared several weeks ahead and refrigerated.

2 cups peeled and cubed fresh horseradish
1 1/2 cups white vinegar
2 tablespoons sugar, or to taste
Pinch of salt
Ground white pepper to taste

Processor Method

1. Insert the shredding disc in the bowl of the food processor. Fill the feed tube with horseradish cubes. With the processor on, use the pusher to push the cubes through feed tube.

2. Remove the shredding disc and insert the steel blade. Pulse several times to get the consistency you like. Remove the horseradish to a small bowl and add the vinegar, sugar, salt, and pepper. Mix everything well with a fork. Place in a container with a tight-fitting lid and refrigerate.

Conventional Method

Peel a large piece of the horseradish root. Use a grater to grate the horseradish. Place in a bowl and add the vinegar, sugar, salt, and pepper. Mix well with a fork. Place in a container with a tight-fitting lid and refrigerate.

Matzo Products
Matzos for table

Dairy and Eggs
Large eggs (1 for the Ashkenazic recipe;
8 for the Sephardic)

Vegans substitute beets, avocado pits,
or potatoes for the eggs

Fish, Meat, and Poultry
1 lamb shank bone or 1 chicken wing

Vegetarians/vegans substitute a mushroom
for the shank bone

Vegetables
Horseradish root

Parsley or celery

Romaine lettuce

One 8-ounce jar horseradish or
freshly grated horseradish root

Fruit and Nuts:
For the Ashkenazic Charoset
1 cup chopped nuts (walnuts, pecans,
almonds, or a mixture)

5 small apples

1 lemon

Fruit and Nuts:
For the Sephardic Charoset
8 ounces pitted dates

4 ounces golden raisins

4 ounces dark raisins

1 Granny Smith apple

4 ounces blanched slivered almonds

1 orange

Herbs, Spices, and Flavorings
Parsley or celery

Ground cinnamon

Ground ginger

White pepper

Salt

Staples
Sugar

White vinegar

Beverages, Wine, and Spirits
Sweet wine for the charoset

Wine and/or grape juice

PREPARATION TIMETABLE

Two or three days before the Seder

Roast the lamb shank (or chicken wing if using). Cover well and refrigerate.

Prepare or purchase the horseradish and refrigerate it.

Cut up individual pieces of the parsley, celery, or romaine lettuce. Place in a zip-top bag or sealed container in the refrigerator.

Hard-boil and roast the egg(s). Cover and refrigerate.

Make the Sephardic charoset, cover, and refrigerate.

A day before the Seder

Prepare the salt water and refrigerate.

Prepare the Seder plate. Cover it well with plastic wrap and aluminum foil, then refrigerate it.

On the day of the Seder

Make the Ashkenazic charoset, cover well with plastic wrap and aluminum foil, and refrigerate.

Three hours before your Seder ceremony begins

Place the Seder plate and extra ceremonial foods on the table.

THE SEDER FESTIVE MEALS

Six complete menus to choose from! See chapter 2 for information on recipe ingredients and food products designated kosher for Passover.

An Ashkenazic Seder

Let all who are hungry come in and eat,

let all who are needy come and make Passover.

—The Haggadah

This Seder menu is the most familiar and popular. The term *Ashkenazic* originally meant "German." Today it refers to the culture, folklore, social institutions, and people of central and eastern Europe, including their descendants.

Those following Ashkenazic Passover traditions do not eat peas or beans or prepare foods made with grains such as wheat, rye, oats, barley, corn, or rice; these grains are similar to those that are used to bake bread. These communities used potatoes, which are permitted, as a staple.

CEREMONIAL FOODS
FOR THE SEDER PLATE

(See chapter 3 for menu and recipes.)

FESTIVE MEAL MENU

Appetizer
Bess Paper's Gefilte Fish

First Course
Grandmother Jacob's Chicken Soup
with Matzo Balls

Salad
Watercress Mushroom Salad
with Balsamic Vinaigrette Dressing

Entrée
Braised Shoulder Roast in Red Wine

Side Dishes
Rosemary Roasted Potatoes

Julienne Vegetables

Desserts
Sylvia Levin's Passover Sponge Cake

Kiwi-Mint Sorbet

Beverages
Coffee, tea, and soft drinks

Suggested Wines
Baron Herzog Chardonnay (appetizer)

Baron Herzog Red Zinfandel,
Yarden Cabernet, or Merlot (entrée)

Herzog Johannisberg Riesling
or Yarden Port Blanc (dessert)

Bess Paper's Gefilte Fish

Makes 30 to 36 fish balls

Preparing gefilte fish was a challenge I couldn't resist. I called one of the best Jewish cooks I know in Cincinnati, my friend Bess Paper. Because this traditional recipe takes time, I make it only twice a year, Passover and Rosh Hashanah. I always make plenty so family and friends can take some home.

When ordering your fish, tell the store to wrap the fish frames, or skeletal part, heads, and trimmings in a separate package. These add flavor to the fish stock. In most large cities, if you ask, the fishmonger will grind the fish for you. Should you have to grind it yourself, Bess says, "Don't grind it too fine. If you stick your finger into the ground fish, some of the fish should adhere to your finger, and it should be the consistency of fine hamburger."

5 pounds whole whitefish

2 pounds whole pike or trout

2 quarts cold water, or enough to cover the fish

1 tablespoon salt (approximately)

4 teaspoons sugar

Freshly ground black pepper to taste

4 large onions

4 carrots

4 large eggs

1/4 to 1/2 cup cold club soda

1 cup matzo meal

1. Rinse the fish frames, head, skin, and trimmings under cold water. Place them in a double layer of cheesecloth and set them in the bottom of a large stockpot. Add the water, 2 teaspoons salt, 1 teaspoon sugar, and some freshly ground pepper. Bring to a boil over high heat. Skim off the foam that accumulates on the top. Slice 2 of the onions and 2 of the carrots and add them to the boiling water. Turn the heat down to low. Cover and allow to simmer while preparing the fish balls.

2. If the fish has been ground, you can skip to step 3. Otherwise, cut the fish fillets into 1-inch pieces. With the steel blade in place, place the fish pieces in the bowl of your food processor. Pulse several times, then process for 15 seconds. This may need to be done in several batches. Empty the ground fish into a large mixing bowl. Make sure you don't grind the fish too fine.

3. Quarter the remaining 2 carrots, and slice the remaining 2 onions. Place them in the food processor bowl and process them until finely chopped. Add these to the ground fish. Mix well.

4. To the addition, add 1 egg at a time, mixing well after each. Mix in the remaining fish, sugar, salt, a little more ground pepper, the club soda, and the matzo meal. The consistency should be a light, soft mixture that holds its shape.

5. Remove the fish frames from the simmering stock and discard. Fill a medium-size bowl with cold water. Dip your hands into the water, and scooping

continues

up about 1/4 cup of fish, form the mixture into an oval shape. Gently place in the simmering stock. Continue until all the fish mixture is in the pot.

6. Cover the pot and reduce the heat to low. Allow the fish balls to cook in the simmering stock for 1 hour 30 minutes. Check and shake the pot every once in a while so the fish balls don't stick together. With a slotted spoon, remove the fish balls to a separate container. Pour a little stock over the fish and add some sliced carrots. Cover well with plastic wrap and chill until ready to serve.

Note: You may wish to strain the remaining fish stock and freeze it to make chowder at a later date.

What's the "Gefilte" in Gefilte Fish?

We find the first biblical reference to fish in Genesis and the story of the Creation. "And God blessed them, saying: 'Be fruitful and multiply and fill the waters in the seas . . .'" According to ancient legend, the fish would come to the righteous of Israel in the form of a giant fish from the sea, the Leviathan.

Over the past twenty or twenty-one centuries, Jews have been preparing Sabbath meals that almost always include fish. The Sabbath laws, set down by the great rabbis eighteen hundred years ago to remind the Jews of the wondrousness of the creations of God, stated that acts of human creativity were not allowed, prohibiting Jews from preparing food on the Sabbath and, especially, separating the wheat from the chaff (referred to as winnowing). This was extended to all human creativity and work in which separation was involved, including cooking and baking. To the most observant Orthodox Jews, eating a fish in which the bones are still intact and need to be removed is considered a form of separation and therefore is prohibited.

The answer came in the creation of a boneless piece of fish, which could be prepared before the Sabbath and enjoyed because it didn't contain any bones. The first recipe, of Roman origin, called for steaming a mixture of boned, chopped fish, pepper, a strong herb called rue, fish broth, and raw eggs.

The Yiddish name given to this type of recipe was *gefilte* (geh-FILL-teh), or "stuffed fish." The recipes originated with the Jews of Germany and Rumania. The German Jewish recipe consisted of golf-ball-sized pieces of ground and heavily spiced freshwater fish, which were boiled in a fish broth and usually served chilled.

The Rumanian Jewish recipe gutted a large freshwater fish and removed all the flesh, leaving the skin and head intact. Then they removed the bones, mixed the flesh with spices and flour, and stuffed it back inside. The fish was sewn closed, baked, and served "whole." Hence the name *gefilte*.

GRANDMOTHER JACOB'S CHICKEN SOUP WITH MATZO BALLS

MAKES 12 TO 14 SERVINGS

Chicken soup is known the world over as Jewish penicillin. This recipe has been in my mother's family since I was a small child. My father, of blessed memory, was my first cooking teacher. Early in my marriage, I remember him stopping by my apartment, walking into my kitchen, lifting up the lid on the chicken soup and saying, "You need more salt."

Whenever I make chicken soup, I use only kosher chickens because they're free of additives and give better flavor to the soup. Ask the butcher to cut the chicken into 8 pieces for you and to include the giblets. I always make extra for the freezer because you never know when you'll catch cold. The soup and chicken can be frozen separately for later use.

One 4- to 5-pound stewing chicken (with giblets),
   cut into 8 pieces
3 whole cloves
1 large onion
1 large parsnip
Several sprigs fresh parsley
2 ribs celery, with leaves on
1 teaspoon salt
1/4 teaspoon gound white pepper
Matzo Balls (see recipe, page 30)

1. Rinse the chicken pieces in cold water. Make sure all the pinheads (ends of the feathers) are removed. Place the chicken in a large stockpot along with the giblets. Do not put the heart or the liver in the pot. Add enough cold water to cover the chicken, about 12 cups. Place the lid on the pot and bring to a boil. Skim the foam as it rises to the surface. Turn the heat down low to simmer.

2. Stick the cloves into the whole onion. Add this to the pot with the parsnip, parsley, celery, salt, and pepper. Cover the pot and simmer slowly for 2 to 3 hours.

3. Use a slotted spoon to remove the chicken and giblets to a large bowl. Save the chicken for another use (see note below). Discard the onion, celery, parsley, and parsnip. Pour the broth through a sieve or fine strainer and discard any solids. Cover and refrigerate the broth and chicken overnight. To serve, remove the congealed fat from the top of the soup. Pour the soup into a large pot and warm over medium heat. Add the matzo balls. Warm for 15 minutes and serve.

Note: You may wish to remove the chicken from the bones and use it for chicken salad or recipes calling for cooked chicken.

continues

MATZO BALLS

MAKES 12 LARGE OR 18 SMALL
MATZO BALLS

This foolproof recipe belonged to my husband's Great Aunt Lizzie from Baltimore. She was an absolutely fantastic cook. If you like matzo balls that are light, melt in your mouth, and float, you'll love these. What makes the matzo balls float is whipping air into the egg whites and then folding them gently into the yolks so the mixture does not break down.

3 large eggs, separated
1/4 teaspoon salt
Pinch of ground white pepper
1/8 teaspoon ground cinnamon
3/4 cup matzo meal

1. In a medium bowl, combine the egg yolks, salt, pepper, and cinnamon.

2. In a small bowl, using a portable mixer, beat the egg whites until they hold nice soft peaks. Using a rubber spatula, fold them gently into the egg yolk mixture.

3. Gently fold in the matzo meal 1/4 cup at a time; it should be absorbed but still hold air and not become thick like paste. You may not need the entire 3/4 cup; it all depends on the size of the yolks. Cover and refrigerate for 15 minutes.

4. Partially fill a large pot with water and bring to a boil. Remove the matzo ball mixture from the refrigerator. Moisten your hands with cold water, then take 1/4 to 1/2 cup of the mixture into your wet hands. Form it into a ball and drop it into the boiling water. When all the matzo balls are in the pot, reduce heat to low and simmer, covered, for about 45 minutes.

5. Remove the matzo balls with a slotted spoon to a large bowl. When cool, add them to the chicken soup. Simmer in the soup for 15 minutes before serving.

Note: Matzo balls can be made 1 or 2 days ahead and kept in the refrigerator. For a little color, I add 1/4 teaspoon chopped fresh parsley to the egg yolk mixture. Matzo balls can be used in any type of broth or served hot as a substitute for potatoes.

WATERCRESS MUSHROOM SALAD
WITH BALSAMIC VINAIGRETTE DRESSING

MAKES 8 SERVINGS

To me, watercress is refreshing, spicy, and reminds me of spring. If watercress isn't to your liking, substitute a variety of lettuces such as Boston, red leaf, and celery cabbage. When making any type of tossed salad for a large crowd, I put it together several hours before I need it, using a technique I learned in a cooking class I took from Molly O'Neill, food writer for the *New York Times Magazine*. You place a smaller amount of dressing than you think you'll need in the bottom of a large salad bowl. Then begin layering the greens, starting with the heaviest type on the bottom and ending with the more fragile ones on top. All the other ingredients—in this case, the sliced mushrooms and orange segments—are added last. Cover the bowl well with plastic wrap, then refrigerate. Toss just before serving. The greens will be crisp and the salad won't be wet.

4 bunches watercress
1 pound mushrooms, sliced
2 navel oranges, peeled and sectioned
Balsamic Vinaigrette Dressing

1. Rinse the watercress well. Tear the leaves off any of the thicker stems and discard the stems. Tear the smaller stems in half. Dry the leaves on paper towels, then wrap the watercress in a dish towel and refrigerate until ready to serve. If using a variety of lettuces, follow Molly O'Neill's technique.

2. When ready to serve, place the watercress on a plate. Garnish with mushroom slices and orange sections. Pass additional dressing separately.

BALSAMIC VINAIGRETTE DRESSING

MAKES APPROXIMATELY 2 CUPS

1 1/4 cups olive oil
2 1/2 tablespoons balsamic vinegar
2 tablespoons freshly squeezed
   lemon juice
3 tablespoons semidry red wine
Salt and freshly ground black
   pepper to taste

In a small bowl, blend all the ingredients together using a wire whisk.

BRAISED SHOULDER ROAST IN RED WINE

MAKES 8 SERVINGS

This roast needs to marinate two days before it is placed in the oven. The marinade is also great on other types of roasts. I tried it on a brisket, which turned out fabulous. Any leftover gravy can be frozen or used at another time, over meatballs or meat loaf.

3 whole cloves

1/4 cup ketchup

4 ribs celery, thinly sliced

3 cups dry red wine

Salt and freshly ground black pepper
   to taste

4 carrots, sliced

1/2 teaspoon ground nutmeg

2 medium onions, sliced

5 large cloves garlic, thinly sliced

4 sprigs fresh thyme, or 1 tablespoon
   dried

2 whole bay leaves

2 sprigs fresh rosemary, or 2 teaspoons
   dried

One 3- to 4-pound beef shoulder roast

Matzo cake meal for coating the roast

6 tablespoons olive oil

1. Place all the ingredients except the roast, cake meal, and olive oil in a rectangular 9×13-inch glass baking dish. Stir, add the roast, cover, and refrigerate for 2 days, turning the roast occasionally.

2. Remove the roast from the marinade and wipe it dry with paper towels. Coat the roast on all sides with the cake meal and set aside.

3. Place the marinade liquid and vegetables in a large saucepan. Bring to a boil, lower the heat to medium, and cook until the marinade is reduced by half, about 20 minutes.

4. Heat the oil in the bottom of a large Dutch oven. When the oil sizzles after a drop of water is added, put in the roast and sear it on all sides, 10 to 15 minutes.

5. Pour the reduced marinade over the roast. Bring to a boil, then reduce the heat to simmer. Cover the roast and cook for 3 to 4 hours, or until fork-tender.

6. Remove the roast from the pan, and allow it to rest while preparing the gravy. Place the liquid and vegetables remaining in the pan into the bowl of a food processor or into a blender. Process or blend until you have a smooth pureed gravy. Cut the meat into 1/2-inch slices. Warm the gravy, pour it over the sliced meat, and serve.

Note: If the finished gravy is too thick, you can add a little stock, water, or dry red wine to thin it out.

ROSEMARY ROASTED POTATOES

This is a great accompaniment for poultry or beef. If you don't care for rosemary, substitute another fresh herb, like thyme or oregano. Try not to use dried herbs; it's the fresh herb that gives these potatoes their distinctive flavor. You may wish to add some minced garlic or onion to the olive oil.

2 pounds small red new potatoes
2 tablespoons olive oil
2 teaspoons fresh rosemary
Salt and freshly ground black pepper
    to taste

1. Preheat the oven to 400°F. Wash the potato skins with a soft brush. Cut the potatoes in half. Place them in rows in the bottom of a medium ovenproof dish. Brush them with olive oil, turning to coat each half.

2. Sprinkle the potatoes with rosemary, salt, and pepper. Bake the potatoes for 30 to 45 minutes, stirring occasionally. If the potatoes are tender when pierced with a fork, they are ready to be served.

JULIENNE VEGETABLES

The vegetables can be steamed ahead and reheated with the remaining ingredients just before serving.

4 medium zucchini

2 ribs celery

5 medium carrots, peeled

1/2 teaspoon salt

6 tablespoons margarine or butter

1 tablespoon freshly squeezed
    lemon juice

1/4 teaspoon ground nutmeg

Pinch of sugar

Pinch of ground white pepper

Microwave Method

1. Cut the zucchini, celery, and carrots to fit the feed tube of your food processor. Insert the julienne or French-fry disc. Stack the vegetables vertically and push with medium pressure.

2. Place the julienned vegetables in a 4-quart microwave-safe baking dish with 1/2 cup water. Cook on high for 5 minutes. Remove the vegetables and place them in a colander. Rinse them under cold running water to stop the cooking.

3. Combine the salt, margarine, lemon juice, nutmeg, sugar, and pepper in a 2-cup, microwave-safe container. Microwave on high for 45 seconds. Stir into the vegetables and microwave on warm for 1 to 2 minutes or until heated through. Serve.

Conventional Method

1. Cut the zucchini, celery, and carrots into small, thin strips using a sharp knife. Steam them in a steamer basket set in a large saucepan for about 10 minutes. Remove the vegetables and place them in a colander. Rinse them under cold running water to stop the cooking.

2. Preheat the oven to 400°F. Place the remaining ingredients in a medium saucepan over medium-high heat. Cook until the margarine melts. Pour into an 8×10-inch baking pan and add the vegetables. Warm in the oven for 5 minutes. Serve.

SYLVIA LEVIN'S PASSOVER SPONGE CAKE

MAKES 12 TO 14 SERVINGS

Sylvia and Morry Levine were our neighbors for more than 25 years. The first year we moved in, Sylvia brought her sponge cake over as a Passover gift. She passed away several years ago, but I continue to serve her sponge cake at my Seders.

10 large eggs, separated
1 heaping cup sugar
Juice and grated zest of 2 lemons
1/3 cup matzo cake meal
1/3 cup potato starch

1. Preheat the oven to 350°F. Make sure the mixing bowl from your mixer is very clean. Beat the egg whites on medium until soft peaks form. Add the sugar about 2 tablespoons at a time and continue beating on high until the egg whites become stiff but not dry. In a separate bowl, beat the egg yolks, lemon juice, and zest together well. Turn the mixer to medium speed and add the egg yolk mixture to the egg whites.

2. Into a small bowl, sift the matzo cake meal and potato starch together. Turn the mixer to low speed and add the sifted meal. Pour the batter into an ungreased tube pan, such as an angel food cake pan. Bake for 1 hour. Invert the tube pan over the narrow neck of a bottle so that air gets underneath the cake. Allow the cake to cool about 30 minutes before removing it from the pan.

TIPS TO KEEP YOUR CAKE FROM FALLING

- Have the eggs at room temperature.

- Use only large eggs.

- Don't add sugar until the egg whites begin to hold small soft peaks.

- Beat the egg whites until good and stiff but not dry.

- Never make a sponge cake on a wet day.

KIWI-MINT SORBET

MAKES 1 QUART

This refreshing dessert tastes like spring. I adapted it from a recipe my Cincinnati friend Melissa Lanier gave me.

2/3 cup water

2/3 plus 1/2 cup sugar

3 kiwis, peeled and sliced

1 tablespoon grated orange zest

1/4 cup fresh mint leaves

1 cup heavy cream or 1 large egg white

1. In a medium saucepan, combine the water and 2/3 cup of the sugar. Cook over medium-high heat, stirring constantly with a wooden spoon, until the sugar melts and you have a thick syrup, 5 to 10 minutes. Or you can do this in a microwave oven in a 4-cup glass measure for 3 to 5 minutes on high. Let the sugar syrup cool.

2. In a food processor or blender, place the kiwi, orange zest, remaining 1/2 cup sugar, and mint leaves and process for 15 seconds. With the machine running, pour the cooled sugar syrup through the feed tube. Process everything for 5 more seconds.

3. Empty the mixture into a medium metal bowl and cover with plastic wrap. Freeze for 3 to 4 hours or overnight.

4. Several hours before serving, remove the sorbet from the freezer. Loosen the sorbet from the metal bowl with a dinner knife and cut into several pieces. Place the pieces into the processor bowl or blender and pulse several times until smooth. Add the heavy cream and process until light and fluffy, 10 to 15 seconds. Empty the sorbet back into the metal bowl. Cover well with plastic wrap, and keep in the freezer until ready to serve.

Matzo Products

Matzos

Matzo cake meal

Matzo meal

Dairy and Eggs

1/2 pint heavy cream

1 1/2 dozen large eggs

4 ounces margarine

Fish, Meat, and Poultry

5 pounds whole whitefish

2 pounds whole pike or trout

3- to 4-pound beef shoulder roast

4- to 5-pound stewing chicken with giblets

Vegetables

2 bunches carrots

1 bunch celery

1 pound mushrooms

7 large onions

1 large parsnip

2 pounds small red new potatoes

4 bunches watercress

4 medium zucchini

Fruits and Nuts

3 kiwis

4 large lemons

3 navel oranges

Herbs, Spices, and Flavorings

Bay leaves

Ground cinnamon

Whole cloves

1 head garlic

Mint leaves

Ground nutmeg

1 bunch parsley

Black peppercorns

Ground white pepper

Fresh rosemary

Salt

Thyme, fresh or dried

Staples

Ketchup

Olive oil

Potato starch

Sugar

Balsamic vinegar

Beverages, Wine, and Spirits

Club soda

Dry red wine

Semidry red wine

Table wine

Grape juice

Coffee, tea, and soft drinks

PREPARATION TIMETABLE

Things you can prepare a week or two ahead

Make the fish stock and grind the fish fillets.

Freeze the fish stock and ground fish in separate containers.

Prepare the soup and refrigerate overnight, remove the congealed fat, and place soup in the freezer until ready to reheat and serve.

Complete the sorbet and place it in the freezer until ready to serve.

Mix the vinaigrette dressing and refrigerate. Bring to room temperature before adding it to the salad.

Two or three days before the Seder

Prepare the marinade and marinate the beef shoulder roast in a deep container for two days, turning it now and then. After two days, cook the roast. Separate the roast from the gravy and refrigerate.

Defrost fish stock and ground fish. Prepare the gefilte fish. Wrap well and refrigerate.

Cut the zucchini, carrots, and celery into julienne strips. Place these in a resealable plastic bag and refrigerate.

A day before the Seder

Bake the cake. Set on a serving platter. Cover well.

On the day of the Seder

Roast the potatoes. When they are done, remove them from the oven, cover them well, and refrigerate until ready to warm before serving.

Slice the mushrooms for the salad, wrap in paper towels, and refrigerate.

Steam the vegetables, season, cover, and refrigerate.

Three hours before your Seder ceremony begins

Place extra matzos, wine, horseradish, and charoset on the table. Fill the wine glasses for the first cup. Prepare salad and refrigerate.

Slice the gefilte fish. Set on serving plates, cover, and refrigerate.

Slice the roast, prepare the gravy, and place in the baking dish. Refrigerate.

One hour before serving the festive meal

Preheat the oven to 250°F. Place the roasted potatoes and shoulder roast in the oven, covered, to warm.

Heat the soup on top of the stove on the lowest setting.

Just before you sit down to begin the festive meal

Warm the vegetables on the stove or in a microwave just before serving.

Remove the sorbet from the freezer and place in the refrigerator.

A SEPHARDIC SEDER

And you shall tell your children on that day

saying, this is on account of what the Eternal

did for me, when I went forth from Egypt.

For the Lord redeemed not only our ancestors,

He redeemed us with them.

—Exodus 13:8

Sephardic is an adjective meaning "Spanish." The Sephardic Jews and their descendants lived in Spain and Portugal until their expulsion in 1492. Today when we speak of *Sephardim* (plural), we include Jews from Turkey, Greece, the Balkans, Italy, and Israel. North African Jews and Jews from Arab countries, though not part of the Spanish expulsion, also follow Sephardic customs.

Most holiday and Sabbath meals begin with several cold appetizers similar to the Italian *antipasto,* only each appetizer is passed in its own serving dish. These are referred to as *salada,* or salads. As in most European traditions, the Sephardic custom is to serve the salad after the entrée, to cleanse the palate for dessert. Sephardic festive meals include eight to ten different salads, each one a culinary adventure. You needn't prepare them all; two or three will suffice.

I was introduced to the beautiful customs, exotic spices, and fabulous food of the Sephardic world by my neighbor and friend Mireille Gabbour, who spent her childhood in Morocco. I have tried to include a variety of Sephardic recipes in this festive dinner menu, several of Mireille's and several from other members of the Cincinnati Sephardic community.

CEREMONIAL FOODS FOR THE SEDER PLATE

(See chapter 3 for menu and recipes.)

FESTIVE MEAL MENU

Appetizers
Allegria Cohen's Chizu Salada
(Carrot Salad)

Allegria Cohen's Spinach Salad

Roasted Aubergine
(Eggplant)

Sephardic Salade Shackshooka
(Marinated Roasted Bell Peppers)

Oriental Salada

Radish Rosettes

First Course
La Soupe de Pesach
(Vegetable Soup for Passover)

Second Course
Moroccan Baked Salmon with Carrots

Entrée
Middle East Lamb Shoulder
with Saffron and Herbs

Side Dishes
Artichoke Bottoms Filled with
Green Peas and Mushrooms

Sonal's Basmati Rice

Salad
La Salada Vert
(Green Salad)

Moroccan Sweets
Dad's Compote de Fruta Seca
(Hot Fruit Compote)

Moroccan Stuffed Dates

Almond Macaroons

Beverages
Moroccan Tea

Coffee, tea, and soft drinks

Suggested Wines
Yarden Sauvignon Blanc or Chardonnay
(appetizer/fish course)

Rothchild Bordeaux or
Herzog Reserved Cabernet
(entrée)

Herzog Late Harvest
Johannisberg Riesling
(dessert)

GUIDE TO SEPHARDIC SPICES

BLACK PEPPER:

Freshly ground peppercorns adds zest and warmth to many savory dishes.

CAPERS:

These are the pickled flower buds of a Mediterranean shrub. They are packed in brine, so it is important to rinse and drain them before using. Refrigerate the jar after opening.

CARDAMOM:

These come whole in pods but can also be purchased in seed form. Cardamom is expensive, but its strong flavor means that a little bit goes a long way. The seeds need to be ground before using. Whole cardamom pods can be added to a variety of dishes.

CAYENNE PEPPER:

This is finely ground dried hot red peppers. A pinch is usually all you need. In order to get the best flavor, add cayenne when you start cooking a dish, sautéing it with other primary seasonings.

CHILIES:

Fresh chili peppers add more than heat. They give zest to a dish. The jalapeño pepper is the most popular, but there is a wide selection of peppers, ranging from fiery to mellow. Taste a tiny piece before deciding how much to add during cooking.

Fresh chilies can be kept in the vegetable drawer of your refrigerator for weeks. If you prefer dried chilies, it is advisable to grind them fine or coarse, whichever you desire.

CILANTRO (FRESH CORIANDER):

Cilantro has a significant fresh fragrance and unique flavor. It's great in salsa, soups, marinades, sauces, and stews. It is best to add the chopped fresh leaves at the end of cooking.

CINNAMON:

Cinnamon is universally popular. In Sephardic cooking, cinnamon is used as a fragrant spice in savory soups, stews, and sauces rather than in baking.

CLOVES:

Cloves need to be handled with a light hand. Too much in the dish can overpower it and ruin it. Its spicy flavor brings out the best in curries and desserts.

CUMIN:

Cumin's robust flavor seems to be the spice of choice for a myriad of Sephardic dishes. It helps to roast the whole seeds for a couple of minutes in a dry skillet or a toaster oven before grinding. Cumin is also available already ground.

continues

GARLIC:

Garlic is the most popular seasoning. It is best to use fresh garlic cloves. The bulbs or heads of garlic should be firm and solid, with no brown spots or soft sections. Choose heads with large cloves. Do not store them in the refrigerator.

PAPRIKA:

Sephardic cooks prefer hot paprika, but the sweet Hungarian paprika is more to my liking, and if you're already using cayenne, you don't need hot paprika.

SAFFRON:

Saffron is made from the dried stamens of the saffron crocus. It is quite expensive and should be purchased in strand, not powdered, form. You can grind it yourself. It gives an intriguing flavor and beautiful gold color to savory dishes.

ALLEGRIA COHEN'S CHIZU SALADA

(CARROT SALAD)

MAKES 8 SERVINGS

Mireille's mother, Allegria, is a caterer. Whenever she visits Cincinnati, she shares her Sephardic cooking expertise with me. This Sephardic salad will give your palate a surprise. Though piquant, it will keep in the refrigerator for up to 1 week. Allegria told me, "The size of the carrots must be that of a princess's finger. And don't cook them too soft or too crunchy." Look for bags of baby carrots, already peeled and cleaned, in the produce section of your supermarket. Of course, regular carrots cut into 1/4-inch-wide slices also work.

2 pounds peeled baby carrots

2 teaspoons ground cumin

1/2 teaspoon paprika

1 teaspoon salt

1/4 teaspoon dried red pepper flakes
    or ground red pepper

Juice of 1 large lemon

2 tablespoons olive oil

Chopped fresh parsley for garnish

1. Place the carrots in a medium saucepan. Cover with cold water and cook over medium heat until the tip of a knife can pierce them, about 15 minutes. Do not overcook. Drain and let cool.

2. In a small bowl, mix cumin, paprika, salt, red pepper flakes, lemon juice, and olive oil together. Add this to the cooked carrots and gently coat them. Let cool for 20 minutes. Garnish with the parsley. These may be prepared up to 1 week before the Seder. Serve at room temperature.

Note: The carrots can be cooked in a microwave-safe dish. Add 1/3 cup cold water to the carrots, cover, and microwave on high for approximately 8 minutes.

ALLEGRIA COHEN'S SPINACH SALAD

MAKES 8 SERVINGS

This Sephardic salad is called *slk* (pronounced "silk") and is traditionally served on the Sabbath. It is a favorite of mine.

*Five 10-ounce packages frozen leaf or
    chopped spinach*

1/4 cup olive oil

6 cloves garlic, minced

1 1/2 tablespoons salt

1 tablespoon ground cumin

1 teaspoon paprika

1 teaspoon cayenne pepper

Juice of 2 lemons

Lemon slices for garnish (optional)

1. Place the frozen spinach in a large bowl, cover with boiling water, and let stand for 20 to 30 minutes. Drain off the water and press out all the excess liquid. If using leaf spinach, cut it into small pieces.

2. Heat the oil in a large skillet. Add the garlic, and stir-fry over medium heat until the garlic is soft and has a glazed look, about 1 minute. Do not let it turn brown.

3. Add the spinach and sauté for 1 or 2 more minutes. Add the salt, cumin, paprika, cayenne, and lemon juice. Mix well. Lower the heat, and cook, stirring occasionally, until all the liquid has evaporated.

4. Refrigerate. You can prepare this several days ahead. Garnish with slivers of lemon peel or lemon slices. Serve at room temperature.

*Note: Another method of removing the excess
    liquid from the spinach is to wrap the
    cooked spinach in 2 paper towels or a dish
    towel and twist. The excess liquid releases
    quickly.*

ROASTED AUBERGINE

(EGGPLANT)

MAKES 6 SERVINGS

Small Asian eggplants are best for this Sephardic appetizer. A small purple globe eggplant can also be used. You may wish to quarter some of the larger eggplant slices. The Sephardic method has the eggplant immersed in vinegar and herbs. I prefer the modern method of salting the eggplant, which allows it to absorb less fat and makes the eggplant softer. I salt the eggplant, cover it with aluminum foil, and weigh it down by setting a heavy pan on top of the foil.

2¹/2 pounds eggplant (8 to 10 small
    eggplants)

2 tablespoons kosher salt

Cooking spray for pans

2 tablespoons olive oil, plus extra for
    coating the eggplant

4 large cloves garlic, finely chopped

1 cup finely chopped fresh parsley

2 tablespoons freshly squeezed
    lemon juice

1. Cut off the stem end of each eggplant. Score the eggplants in strips lengthwise with a vegetable peeler. Then cut into 1/2-inch rounds. Place in a 9×13-inch baking dish.

2. Sprinkle with the salt and add enough water to barely cover the tops. Cover with foil. Place a heavy plate or lid on top to weigh the eggplant down. Allow to stand for 30 minutes. Drain and dry with paper towels.

3. Preheat the broiler. Coat a jelly roll pan or rimmed baking sheet with cooking spray. Arrange the eggplant slices in a single layer on the pan; lightly brush the tops of the slices with a little oil. Broil a few inches from the heat for approximately 5 minutes. Watch carefully so the eggplant doesn't burn. Turn over the slices and broil for 3 minutes. Place in a shallow casserole.

4. In a small skillet, heat the 2 tablespoons of olive oil over medium-high heat. Add the garlic and half of the parsley and stir-fry for 1 minute. Remove from the heat. Add to the eggplant slices along with the lemon juice and remaining chopped parsley and toss the slices gently to coat them. Refrigerate, covered, until ready to serve. This dish can be prepared several days ahead. Serve at room temperature.

Note: If the interior of the eggplant is too firm,
    bake the eggplant at 400°F for a few min-
    utes until soft.

Sephardic Salade Shackshooka

(MARINATED ROASTED BELL PEPPERS)

MAKES 6 TO 8 SERVINGS

This will keep for up to 1 week in the refrigerator. I freeze the leftovers and add them to cooked rice.

2 large yellow bell peppers

1 large red bell pepper

4 large ripe tomatoes, peeled, or one 12-ounce container cherry tomatoes

3 tablespoons olive oil

6 small cloves garlic, sliced

1/2 teaspoon salt

1 teaspoon paprika

1/4 teaspoon cayenne pepper

1. Preheat the broiler. Place the whole peppers on a baking sheet or heavy aluminum foil. Broil about 6 inches from the heat source, turning often, until the skins are charred on all sides.

2. Remove them from the oven and place them in a brown paper bag. Close the bag and allow the peppers to steam for 5 to 10 minutes.

3. Remove the peppers from the bag. Using a paring knife, remove the skins, stems, ribs, and seeds. Slice the peppers into strips about 1/4 inch wide. Set aside.

4. Cut the large tomatoes into 1-inch cubes or the cherry tomatoes into quarters, removing the seeds. Heat the olive oil in a large skillet over medium heat. Add the tomatoes and stir-fry for 1 minute. Add the garlic and roasted peppers and sauté 5 minutes more. Cover the pan and simmer over low heat for 30 to 45 minutes. Add the salt, paprika, and cayenne. Continue cooking until the peppers have a jamlike quality. Refrigerate, covered, until ready to serve. This dish can be prepared a week before the Seder. Serve at room temperature.

ORIENTAL SALADA

MAKES 8 TO 10 SERVINGS

This reminds me of the Israeli salad I prepare when we have a picnic on Israeli Independence Day in May. Try to use thin cucumbers, which have smaller seeds and are easier to digest. This salad tastes better when completed an hour or two before serving.

1 cucumber, peeled and diced

2 medium tomatoes, diced

1 green bell pepper, diced

1 rib celery, thinly sliced

1/4 cup chopped cilantro

1 small red onion, chopped

1/4 cup chopped fresh parsley

Salt and freshly ground black pepper to taste

2 tablespoons olive oil

Juice of 1 lemon

1. Place the cucumber, tomatoes, green pepper, celery, cilantro, red onion, and parsley in a bowl. Season with salt and pepper. You can prepare the salad to this point and refrigerate it until 2 hours before serving.

2. In a large bowl, mix the oil and lemon juice together. Pour over the vegetables and mix well. Refrigerate covered. Serve cold.

RADISH ROSETTES

MAKES 8 SERVINGS

Whenever my mother, of blessed memory, served cottage cheese, she would use these for decoration. Mireille uses them as an additional salad. I think these radishes are her way of adding an American touch to her menu. A sharp paring knife is important to make the rosettes.

2 bunches large radishes

12 ice cubes and cold water

1. Wash and stem the radishes. With the tip of a paring knife, starting at the top, slice 4 to 6 small openings halfway down the sides of each radish.

2. Fill a large bowl with the ice cubes and cold water. Drop the prepared radishes into the water. Refrigerate several hours or overnight. Remove the radishes, dry with paper towels, and serve in a decorative container.

LA SOUPE DE PESACH

(VEGETABLE SOUP FOR PASSOVER)

MAKES 8 TO 10 SERVINGS

This traditional soup is served the entire week of Passover. I double the recipe, as it freezes very well. I substitute frozen lima beans for Moroccan broad beans; however, if you wish to be more authentic, Moroccan beans can be found in a store that sells Middle Eastern or Greek foods. It helps to have all the vegetables ready and the spices measured in advance.

1/4 cup sunflower oil

2 large (about 2 pounds) beef shank bones
    or top rib with meat

3 small marrow bones

1 medium onion, sliced

3 to 4 ribs celery, with leaves

Two 10-ounce packages frozen
    lima beans

4 large carrots

2 medium white turnips, peeled
    and diced

4 leeks, white and tender green parts,
    cleaned, trimmed, and sliced

5 Idaho potatoes, peeled and diced

1/2 cup chopped fresh parsley

1/2 cup chopped cilantro

1 tablespoon ground saffron

1 teaspoon ground cumin

1 tablespoon kosher salt

1/2 teaspoon freshly ground black pepper

1. Heat the oil in a large stockpot over medium-high heat. Add the beef shanks, marrow bones, onion, and celery and sauté for 10 to 15 minutes. Cover with cold water and bring to boil over medium heat. Cover and reduce the heat to low.

2. Add 1 package of lima beans and the carrots, turnips, leeks, potatoes, parsley, and cilantro. Add the saffron, cumin, salt, and pepper, and enough water to cover the vegetables and meat, 6 to 8 cups. Put the lid back on and simmer for 2 to 2 1/2 hours or until the meat and vegetables are soft.

3. Remove the meat and bones to a bowl and save for another use (see note below). Remove the vegetables to a food processor or blender and puree. Return the pureed vegetables to the soup pot and add the remaining package of lima beans. Taste for seasonings; you may wish to add more salt and pepper. Cover and bring to a boil; reduce heat to low and simmer for another 30 minutes.

Note: I discard the marrow bones, remove the meat from the beef shanks, and freeze it for later use as a meat filling for Blintzes, Blintzes, and More Blintzes (page 142).

MOROCCAN BAKED SALMON WITH CARROTS

MAKES 8 SERVINGS

Because this is not an entrée but the fish course, it's served in smaller portions. You can prepare it a day or two ahead, then broil just before serving. The spiced oil needs to be prepared a day or two before the salmon is marinated. The spiced oil is what gives the fish its distinctive Moroccan flavor.

SPICED OIL

4 cloves garlic

1 teaspoon chopped red bell pepper

1 teaspoon salt

1/2 teaspoon ground white pepper

1 teaspoon dried red pepper flakes

1/2 cup vegetable oil

1 lemon, thinly sliced

Grated zest and juice of 1 lemon

1 1/2 tablespoons ground saffron

SALMON

2 pounds salmon fillets, cut into 2-inch-wide strips

2 pounds carrots, thinly sliced

Lemon slices for garnish

1. To make the spiced oil, place the garlic, bell pepper, salt, white pepper, red pepper flakes, oil, lemon slices, lemon zest and juice, and saffron in a 1-quart jar or container with a tight-fitting lid. Cover and shake vigorously. Refrigerate for a day or two.

2. Place the salmon in a large glass or ceramic dish. Pour the spiced oil over the salmon slices and turn to coat evenly. Cover and marinate in the refrigerator for 3 to 4 hours. Place the carrots in the bottom of a 9×13-inch glass or ceramic baking dish. Lay the marinated salmon slices over the carrots. Pour any remaining spiced oil evenly over the top. You can prepare the recipe to this point, cover, and refrigerate 3 to 4 hours ahead.

3. Preheat the oven to 300°F. Add 1 inch of water to the bottom of the casserole. Cover the casserole tightly with aluminum foil and bake for 30 minutes; uncover and broil for 2 to 3 minutes or until the salmon appears to be a little crisp on top. Garnish with lemon slices. Serve at room temperature.

Variation

This salmon is absolutely fabulous served cold. Flake the salmon. In a large bowl, mix 1 pint of yogurt or low-fat sour cream, 1 coarsely grated large cucumber, 1/2 teaspoon lemon juice, 1/4 teaspoon snipped fresh dill, and 1 teaspoon horseradish. Mix with the salmon.

MIDDLE EAST LAMB SHOULDER
WITH SAFFRON AND HERBS

MAKES 6 TO 8 SERVINGS

I adore lamb but my husband doesn't care for it, so I don't prepare it except when we're having guests who like lamb. Passover is one of those times. The first time I tasted this at Mireille's, I thought I'd died and gone to heaven. She adds prunes stuffed with almonds to the finished presentation. Ask the butcher to bone, roll, and tie the shoulder for you.

One 12-ounce package of pitted prunes
1/2 cup blanched whole almonds
1/4 cup sugar
1 teaspoon ground cinnamon
One 5-pound rolled and tied boneless
    lamb shoulder
4 cloves garlic, thinly sliced
1/2 cup chopped fresh parsley
2 tablespoons chopped fresh mint,
    or 1 tablespoon dried
2 tablespoons chopped fresh tarragon,
    or 2 teaspoons dried
1 teaspoon salt
1/4 teaspoon freshly ground black pepper
1/2 cup olive oil
2 medium onions, sliced
Juice of 3 lemons
Pinch of cayenne pepper
1/2 teaspoon ground saffron

1. Stuff each prune with an almond. Place in a small saucepan, add the sugar and cinnamon, and pour in 1 cup of cold water. Cover and simmer over low heat for 10 minutes. Remove from the heat, cover, and refrigerate until needed.

2. Preheat the oven to 250°F. With the tip of a knife, make incisions on the outside of the lamb about 1 inch wide and deep enough to be stuffed. Insert slivers of garlic and some parsley inside of each slit.

3. In a 1-cup measure, mix the mint, tarragon, salt, pepper, and 1/4 cup of the olive oil together. Rub this evenly over the entire surface of the lamb.

4. Place the remaining 1/4 cup olive oil in a shallow roasting pan over medium heat, and heat until hot, about 1 minute. Add onions and sauté until golden brown, 3 to 5 minutes. Add half the lemon juice and the cayenne pepper. Turn the heat to low and simmer for 5 minutes. Turn heat to medium-high, add the lamb shoulder, and sear on all sides.

5. In a small bowl, mix the remaining lemon juice with the saffron and pour it around the lamb, along with the 1 1/2 cups of cold water. Place in the oven and roast, basting occasionally, 30 to 35 minutes per pound (2 1/2 to 3 hours). Add the prunes during the last 15 minutes of roasting. The surface of the lamb should be well browned and the interior still slightly pink. When ready to serve, slice the lamb and place it on a platter, surrounded with the prunes.

ARTICHOKE BOTTOMS FILLED WITH
GREEN PEAS AND MUSHROOMS

MAKES 8 SERVINGS

This recipe, though elegant in appearance, is easy on your time. I use canned artichoke bottoms, fresh mushrooms, and frozen young peas. As easy as 1, 2, 3, it is ready to heat and eat.

Two 13³/4-ounce cans artichoke bottoms
Juice and grated zest of 1 lemon
1/4 cup vegetable oil
1 medium onion, minced
1 cup thinly sliced mushrooms
1 cup dry white wine
1 tablespoon potato starch
1 teaspoon pareve chicken
    soup granules
Salt and freshly ground black pepper
    to taste
One 10-ounce package frozen small
    peas

1. Empty the artichoke bottoms into a colander. Pour boiling water over them to get rid of the canned flavor. Place the artichoke bottoms in a bowl with the lemon juice and zest, turning each one to be sure the lemon juice is distributed. Set aside.

2. Heat the oil in a large skillet over medium-high heat. Add the onion and sauté until soft. Add the mushrooms and sauté 5 more minutes.

3. In a medium saucepan, mix the wine, potato starch, and chicken soup granules together with a wire whisk. Add to the mushroom mixture. Reduce the heat to low and stir continuously until the mixture forms a smooth sauce. Add salt and pepper, remove from the heat, and stir in the frozen peas.

4. Remove the artichoke bottoms from the lemon juice. Slice a very thin piece from the bottom of each artichoke so it stands upright. Fill the centers with the mushroom mixture. Place on an ovenproof platter or foil-lined cookie sheet and refrigerate, covered, until just before serving.

5. Preheat the oven to 350°F. Bake the filled artichoke hearts for 15 minutes or until golden brown. Remove and serve.

SONAL'S BASMATI RICE

Rice is not a prohibited food for Sephardic Jews. My friend and Cincinnati neighbor Sonal Sanghvi shared her recipe with me. This rice keeps for several days in the refrigerator and also freezes well.

3 cups basmati rice

1 tablespoon vegetable oil

1/4 cup margarine

5 whole cardamom pods

1 cup minced onions

1/2 teaspoon ground ginger

1/2 cup golden raisins

1 teaspoon salt

Pinch of saffron

4 1/2 cups water

1. Rinse the rice in a colander under cold water until the cloudiness disappears. In a large, heavy saucepan, heat the oil and margarine over medium-high heat; add the cardamom and sauté for 2 to 3 minutes. Add the onions and ginger and sauté until the onions wilt, 2 to 3 minutes.

2. Stir in the rice and 1 cup of water; add the raisins, salt, and saffron. Stir well. Add 3 1/2 more cups of water, bring to a boil, cover, and simmer over low heat approximately 15 minutes, or until the liquid has been absorbed. Do not stir the rice. Remove from the heat and let stand, covered, for 5 to 10 minutes. If desired, fluff with a fork before serving.

LA SALADA VERT

(GREEN SALAD)

MAKES 8 SERVINGS

Mireille serves the salad before the dessert, as the Europeans do. This is a simple mixture of lettuce and toasted walnuts with a lemon-oil dressing.

4 ounces walnut halves

1 head iceberg lettuce

4 cloves garlic, minced

Juice of 1 lemon

1 teaspoon salt

Freshly ground black pepper to taste

3 tablespoons olive oil

1. Preheat the oven to 375°F. Spread the walnuts out on a jelly roll pan or rimmed baking sheet and toast in the oven for 5 to 8 minutes or until they begin to turn a light golden color.

2. Cut the head of lettuce in half. Discard the yellow heart because it is usually bitter. Tear the remaining lettuce into bite-size pieces and place in a large salad bowl. Sprinkle the walnuts on top. Refrigerate, covered, until ready to serve.

3. In a 1-cup glass measuring cup, mix the garlic, lemon juice, salt, pepper, and olive oil together. Set aside. When ready to serve, pour over the salad and toss.

DAD'S COMPOTE DE FRUTA SECA

(HOT FRUIT COMPOTE)

MAKES ABOUT 1 1/2 QUARTS

This is the recipe my father always made for Rosh Hashanah. All the ingredients are placed in a pot, cooked together, and end up as a finger-lickin' great dessert. This is also delicious as a topping for yogurt or ice cream.

8 ounces dried apricots

8 ounces dried peaches

8 ounces dried pears

1/2 cup golden raisins

1/2 cup dark raisins

1 cup sugar (optional)

1 cinnamon stick

Juice of 1 lemon

Juice and grated zest of 1 orange

1 cup store-bought orange juice

3 cups cold water

1/2 cup blanched slivered almonds
    (optional)

1/4 cup brandy

1. Cut the dried fruits into bite-size pieces. Place in a medium saucepan with the raisins, sugar if desired, cinnamon stick, lemon juice, orange juice (fresh and store-bought), orange zest, and water.

2. Cover and bring to a boil over high heat, then turn the heat to low and simmer slowly until fruit gets soft, 25 to 30 minutes. Check to make sure the fruit mixture doesn't get too thick. You may wish to add extra orange juice or water.

3. While the fruit is cooking, toast the almonds. Preheat the oven to 450°F. Spread out the almonds on a jelly roll pan or rimmed baking sheet and toast in the oven for 5 to 10 minutes.

4. Remove the cooked fruit from the heat. Stir in the brandy and almonds. Allow to cool at least 2 hours to absorb the liquid. Cover and refrigerate. Serve warm or at room temperature.

MOROCCAN STUFFED DATES

MAKES ABOUT 36 DATES

If you wish to fill the centers of the dates with whole toasted blanched almonds, walnut halves, or pecan halves, it is best to purchase pitted dates. I stuff mine, but it isn't necessary. These keep well in an airtight container. Mireille tells me, "During Passover, whenever we have company, we offer a platter of stuffed dates, figs, all types of nuts, and many dried fruits to our guests."

8 ounces pitted dates
1/2 cup freshly squeezed orange juice
1 tablespoon brandy

Place the dates in a small bowl. In a 1-cup measure, mix the orange juice and brandy together. Pour over the dates. Soak for 1 hour. Remove dates from the juice mixture. Fill with nuts if desired and set on a serving plate.

ALMOND MACAROONS

MAKES ABOUT 3 DOZEN

Passover without macaroons is like Rosh Hashanah without sweet honey cake or Thanksgiving without pumpkin pie. Sephardic macaroons use lemon zest for flavoring rather than almond extract. The secret to good macaroons is beating the egg whites just right and not overbaking the cookies.

3 large egg whites
Zest of 1 large lemon
1 cup sugar
1 1/2 cups blanched finely ground almonds
Cooking spray, butter, or margarine
*   for greasing pans*

1. Preheat the oven to 275°F. In an electric mixer, beat the egg whites until they form soft peaks. Add the lemon zest. Gradually add the sugar and beat until the whites are very stiff and shiny but not dry. Fold in the ground almonds.

2. Cover 2 baking sheets with aluminum foil and spray or grease them. Using 2 teaspoons, take a heaping teaspoon of batter in one and scoop it off onto the baking sheet using the other teaspoon. Place the cookies 1 to 1 1/2 inches apart. Repeat with the rest of the dough.

3. Bake for 20 to 30 minutes or until the cookies are firm and slightly brown. Let cool for 5 to 10 minutes before removing the cookies from the baking sheets to a rack. When cool, store in an airtight container.

MOROCCAN TEA

Throughout our trip to Morocco, mint tea prepared with freshly dried peppermint or spearmint leaves was offered to us or available for purchase. Always served in small decorative glasses, it was both soothing and satisfying. Each person sweetened their tea to taste. In some cases, sugar syrup was used as a base and brewed tea leaves were strained and added. Some families pass a separate teapot with boiling water so everyone can decide how strong to make their own tea.

8 scant teaspoons dried peppermint
   or spearmint leaves
8 1/2 cups cold water

In a large saucepan, combine the mint leaves with the cold water. Bring to a boil, then remove from the heat and allow to steep for 5 minutes. Strain into a small teapot, sweeten to taste, and serve hot.

Matzo Products
Matzos

Dairy and Eggs
4 ounces margarine

3 large eggs

Fish, Meat, and Poultry
2 pounds salmon fillets

2 large (about 2 pounds) beef shank bones or top rib meat

3 small marrow bones

5-pound boneless lamb shoulder, rolled and tied

Vegetables
2 pounds baby carrots

4 pounds medium carrots

1 bunch celery

1 cucumber

2$1/2$ pounds (8 to 10 small) eggplants

4 leeks

1 head iceberg lettuce

8-ounce container mushrooms

1 small red onion

6 medium white or yellow onions

1 green bell pepper

2 large red bell peppers

2 large yellow bell peppers

5 Idaho potatoes

2 bunches large radishes

4 large tomatoes or 12 ounces cherry tomatoes

2 medium tomatoes

2 medium white turnips

Two 13$3/4$-ounce cans artichoke bottoms

Two 10-ounce packages frozen lima beans

One 10-ounce package frozen small peas

Five 10-ounce packages frozen leaf or chopped spinach

Fruits and Nuts
1 dozen lemons

2 oranges

8 ounces dried apricots

8 ounces dried peaches

8 ounces dried pears

8 ounces dates, whole or pitted

12 ounces pitted prunes

1/2 cup dark raisins

1 cup golden raisins

1 1/2 cups blanched finely ground almonds

1/2 cup blanched slivered almonds

1/2 cup whole blanched almonds

4 ounces walnut halves

Herbs, Spices, and Flavorings
Ground cinnamon

Cinnamon stick

Whole cardamom

Cayenne pepper

1 large bunch fresh cilantro

Ground cumin

4 heads garlic

Ground ginger

1 bunch fresh mint

Peppermint or spearmint tea leaves

Paprika

2 large bunches fresh parsley

Dried red pepper flakes

Saffron strands

Tarragon, fresh or dried

Black peppercorns

Ground white pepper

Salt, regular and kosher

Pareve chicken soup granules

Staples
Basmati rice

Sugar

Olive oil

Potato starch

Sunflower oil

Vegetable oil

Cooking spray (vegetable or olive oil)

Beverages, Wine, and Spirits
8 ounces orange juice

Brandy

Dry white wine

Table wine

Grape juice

Coffee, tea, and soft drinks

Things you can prepare a week or two ahead

Cook the vegetable soup and freeze it.

Cook the fruit compote; cover and refrigerate or freeze.

Stew the prunes. Cover and refrigerate.

Two or three days before the Seder

The carrot, roasted bell pepper, spinach, and eggplant salads can be prepared, covered, and refrigerated.

Cook the rice and refrigerate it.

Prepare the spice oil for the salmon. Refrigerate.

Stuff the dates. Store in an airtight container.

Bake the macaroons. Store in an airtight container.

Prepare and bake the salmon only. Refrigerate.

One day before the Seder

Cut the radishes, place them in water, and refrigerate overnight.

Prepare the lamb for baking and refrigerate.

Make the dressing for the green salad. Store in an airtight container.

If the soup has been frozen, place it in the refrigerator to thaw.

Scald the artichoke bottoms and place in the refrigerator in the lemon juice.

On the day of the Seder

Arrange all the appetizer salads in their serving dishes. Cover and refrigerate.

Remove the radishes from the water and put them in a serving dish. Cover and refrigerate.

Chop the vegetables for the Oriental Salada. Cover and refrigerate.

Prepare the artichoke filling; fill the artichokes and refrigerate, covered.

Tear the lettuce for the salad. Cover and refrigerate.

Three hours before your Seder ceremony begins

Remove the prunes and fruit compote from the refrigerator.

Bake the lamb.

Arrange the dates and macaroons on a serving platter. Cover.

One hour before serving the festive meal

Warm the soup over low heat.

Place the lamb in a warm oven.

Toss the green salad.

Just before you sit down to begin the festive meal

Finish baking the artichoke bottoms.

Warm the rice in the microwave or covered in a low oven.

Prepare the tea.

Broil the salmon.

An "Off-the-Shelf" Seder

. . . and you shall eat it hurriedly:

it is a Passover offering to the LORD.

—Exodus 12:11

No time to shop? No time to cook? This "off-the-shelf" Seder is the answer for the busy household. The recipes are all "shelf starters" because the main ingredient begins with a packaged or frozen product from the store shelf or freezer. You can enhance these products with your personal touch by adding spices, flavorings, or other on-hand ingredients. Everyone will think you spent days in the kitchen when it took only hours.

Every year, new kosher for Passover products are developed and available. Some "shelf" products may change packaging or not be available. If certification is important to you, check with your rabbi to make sure the products are kosher for Passover.

CEREMONIAL FOODS FOR THE SEDER PLATE

(See chapter 3 for menu and recipes.)

FESTIVE MEAL MENU

Appetizers
Quick Gefilte Fish
(It starts with fish from the jar.)

First Course
Greek Lemon-Chicken Soup
(From box, to pan, to bowl.)

Entrée
Baked Apricot-Ginger Chicken
with Sweet and Sour Sauce
(Sauced and easy to bake.)

Side Dishes
Mikki Frank's Warm Fruit Compote
(From the can to the table in minutes.)

Sweet Potato Timbale with Cranberry Puree
(From can to casserole.)

Dessert
Susan's Lemon Chiffon Cake
with Strawberry Sauce
(Boxed Passover angel food cake makes this a
winner. Passover preserves never tasted so good.)

Beverages
Coffee, tea, and soft drinks

Suggested Wines
Baron Herzog White Zinfandel
(appetizer and first course)

Weinstock Pinot Noir
or Herzog French Selection Merlot (entrée)

Gamla Muscat or Muscat Canelli (dessert)

QUICK GEFILTE FISH

MAKES 8 SERVINGS

Store-bought gefilte fish has undergone radical changes, with many more brands on the shelves. Depending upon your family's taste, you have a large variety to choose from: old-fashioned, sweet, spicy, or all whitefish, just to name a few. No matter what you choose, you will be able to add your own personal touch.

4 ounces fresh whitefish fillets
4 ounces fresh carp fillets
Salt
One 24-ounce jar gefilte fish
2 medium onions, sliced
2 medium carrots, sliced

1. Wash the fresh fish. Lightly salt and place in a small bowl; cover and refrigerate for no less than 30 minutes or up to the next day.

2. Drain the fish broth from the 24-ounce jar into a 3-quart nonreactive saucepan. Add the onions and carrots. Cook over medium heat for 15 minutes.

3. Remove the fish fillets from the refrigerator. Dry them with paper towels and place them in the broth. Cook for 12 to 15 minutes or until the fish flakes easily. Be sure not to overcook the fish. Add the jarred gefilte fish and continue cooking 5 more minutes.

4. Remove the gefilte fish; set aside. Remove the fish fillets and discard. Strain the remaining broth. If using the fish loaf variety of gefilte fish, slice into serving pieces. (If using the fish ball variety, do not slice.) Place the slices or whole fish balls in a serving dish. Pour a little of the broth on top, making sure the fish is covered. Decorate with slices of cooked carrot. Refrigerate, covered, until ready to serve.

GREEK LEMON-CHICKEN SOUP

MAKES 10 SERVINGS

Simply follow the directions for the soup mix on the box. Your personal touch of lemon juice and zest at the proper moment will have your guests thinking you cooked the whole day. Be sure to use the entire contents in the box and do not let the soup boil or the eggs will curdle.

Two 3¹/₂-ounce envelopes egg drop
*   soup mix*
2 large eggs
Juice of 2 lemons
1 teaspoon grated lemon zest
Salt and freshly ground black pepper
*   to taste*

1. Empty the contents of both envelopes into a large saucepan. Add 8 cups of cold water.

2. Stir over high heat until the soup comes to a boil, then reduce heat to low and simmer, 2 to 3 minutes.

3. In a 2-cup measure, beat the eggs with the lemon juice and zest. In a thin stream, gradually add the mixture to the simmering soup, stirring rapidly with a wire whisk. Add salt and pepper to taste.

Variation
Instead of eggs, add the lemon juice and zest to the soup, then just before serving the soup, add a few soup nuts (*mandlen*) on top.

Baked Apricot-Ginger Chicken
with Sweet and Sour Sauce

This recipe calls for chicken breasts only, but if you prefer dark meat, add kosher-for-Passover chicken parts. The soup nuts, or *mandlen,* come in a box and need to be ground into crumbs. I prepare a large jar to keep in my pantry for Passover.

2¹/2 to 3 pounds fresh or frozen boneless,
    skinless chicken breasts (4 whole breasts)
One 1³/4-ounce box soup nuts (mandlen), ground
1 teaspoon ground ginger
¹/2 teaspoon salt
¹/4 teaspoon ground white pepper
2 large eggs, or ¹/2 cup egg substitute
1 teaspoon freshly squeezed lemon juice
One 8-ounce jar apricot preserves
¹/2 cup white wine
2 tablespoons margarine, melted

1. If the chicken is frozen, thaw it overnight in your refrigerator. Rinse and clean the parts with cold water and dry well with paper towels. Preheat the oven to 350°F. Cut the chicken breasts in half.

2. Combine the soup nut crumbs, ginger, salt, and pepper in a shallow dish.

3. Beat eggs in a small bowl with the lemon juice and pour into a pie plate. Dip each chicken part in the egg mixture, then in the crumb mixture. Arrange in a single layer in a 9×13-inch baking pan.

4. In a 1-quart microwave-safe bowl, combine the preserves, wine, and margarine; microwave on high for 3 minutes. Or place in a small saucepan and bring to a boil. Pour over the chicken breasts and bake for 1 hour or until the chicken is crisp. Serve with the Sweet and Sour Sauce.

SWEET AND SOUR SAUCE

This recipe begins with a 19-ounce jar of duck sauce, which comes in several flavors. It is a great flavor enhancer for marinades or dipping sauces. Pour over the baked chicken or pass at the table.

2 cups apricot-peach duck sauce
¹/4 teaspoon ground ginger
¹/4 teaspoon ground cloves
1 tablespoon honey

Microwave Method
Place all the ingredients in a 1-quart microwave-safe dish. Microwave on high for 2 minutes. Stir and microwave 1 more minute. Refrigerate and warm before serving.

Conventional Method
Place all the ingredients in a medium saucepan. Bring to a boil over medium-high heat, stirring occasionally. Remove from the heat. Refrigerate and warm before serving.

MIKKI FRANK'S WARM FRUIT COMPOTE

MAKES 10 TO 12 SERVINGS

This is a favorite at our North Avondale *Chavura's* (HA-VOO-RAH) Break-the-Fast. The greatest thing about this recipe is its staying quality, plus the fact you can double or triple the recipe without affecting the consistency and flavor. It keeps in the refrigerator for up to 3 weeks or in the freezer for up to 3 months. Freeze the drained fruit syrups and use them for a punch base. Be sure the curry label says *mild,* or the curry flavor will be overpowering. If you're not a curry person, cut the amount in half.

Two 20-ounce cans pineapple chunks

One 30-ounce can fruit cocktail

One 16-ounce can purple plums

1/3 cup margarine

3/4 cup light brown sugar

2 teaspoons mild Indian curry powder

One 16-ounce can mandarin orange
    segments, drained, for garnish

Fresh mint leaves for garnish

1. Grease a shallow casserole. Drain the pineapple and fruit cocktail well. Mix them together in the prepared casserole. Set aside.

2. Drain the plums, pit, and cut each half in half. Add to the mixed fruit mixture.

3. In a 1-quart microwave-safe bowl, melt the margarine in the microwave for 1 1/2 minutes on high, or in a small saucepan over medium heat. Remove the margarine from the heat. Add the brown sugar and curry powder. Spread this mixture over the fruit. Do not mix. Allow the fruit to marinate at room temperature for 1 to 2 hours.

4. Preheat the oven to 350°F. Bake the fruit compote, uncovered, for 20 to 30 minutes, stirring occasionally, until the fruit appears thick and has blended together. Remove the compote from the oven and allow it to rest for 10 to 15 minutes. Garnish with drained mandarin orange segments and fresh mint leaves. Serve warm or at room temperature.

SWEET POTATO TIMBALE WITH CRANBERRY PUREE

These are elegant looking and very tasty.

One 17-ounce can sweet potatoes
1 1/2 cups liquid nondairy creamer, warmed
4 large eggs
2 tablespoons brown sugar
3/4 teaspoon salt
3/4 teaspoon ground cinnamon
1/2 teaspoon ground cardamom

CRANBERRY PUREE

One 16-ounce can whole cranberry sauce
1/4 cup water or freshly squeezed
  orange juice
2 tablespoons freshly squeezed
  lemon juice

1. Preheat the oven to 350°F. Cut the sweet potatoes into 1-inch pieces. Place the sweet potatoes in a food processor and pulse several times. Process for 45 seconds or until smooth, stopping once to scrape down the sides of the bowl.

2. Add the warmed creamer, eggs, brown sugar, salt, cinnamon, and cardamom to the sweet potatoes. Pulse 3 or 4 times. Scrape the processor bowl and process 5 seconds longer or until thoroughly blended.

3. Grease or spray a 2- to 2 1/2-quart soufflé dish or round casserole; fill with the sweet potato mixture. Set the casserole dish in a pan of hot water. The water should be about as high as the filling in the casserole.

4. Cover the casserole dish loosely with foil. Bake for about 1 hour 15 minutes or until the tip of a knife comes out clean when inserted into the center. While the timbale is baking, prepare the cranberry puree.

5. Place the cranberry sauce, water or orange juice, and lemon juice in the food processor and process until thick and smooth, about 30 seconds. Transfer to a medium saucepan and stir over medium heat until warm. You can also warm the sauce in your microwave oven; place it in a 1 1/2-quart microwave-safe container and microwave on high for 1 minute, stirring after 30 seconds.

6. Remove the casserole of sweet potatoes from the water bath. Allow it to rest for 10 minutes. Run a knife around the outside edge of the dish and invert it onto a serving platter. Spoon half of the cranberry puree over the top of the timbale and serve, passing the remaining sauce.

Note: The timbale can also be served directly
  from the casserole dish.

SUSAN'S LEMON CHIFFON CAKE WITH STRAWBERRY SAUCE

MAKES 12 TO 14 SLICES

This light, low-cholesterol cake is a Shabbat standard at our niece Susan's house. It has become a favorite at our home too. It doesn't need any frosting. Pass your favorite sauce or serve it along with your favorite ice cream or sorbet. For Passover, I like strawberry sauce on the cake.

One 8.9-ounce box Manischewitz
    angel food cake mix

1 cup water

1/4 cup sugar

3/4 cup vegetable oil

3 large eggs

1/2 teaspoon vanilla extract, or 1 packet
    vanilla sugar

2 tablespoons freshly squeezed
    lemon juice

Grated zest of 1 lemon

1 1/2 teaspoons matzo cake meal

Strawberry Sauce (see recipe, page 68)

1. Preheat the oven to 350°F. There will be 2 bags in the cake mix box. Empty the bag containing the powdered egg whites into the large bowl of an electric mixer. Add the water and mix on low speed until the egg whites are dissolved. Increase the speed slowly. When soft peaks begin to form, add the sugar a little at a time. Beat on high speed for 1 to 2 minutes or until soft peaks form. Set aside.

2. In another large bowl, beat the oil and eggs together for 1 to 2 minutes or until well mixed and light in color. Add the extract or vanilla sugar and lemon juice and zest. Mix well.

3. Add the second bag from the cake mix plus the matzo cake meal to the oil and eggs. Mix on low speed until blended. Fold into the beaten egg whites. Pour the batter into an ungreased angel food cake pan or 9-inch tube pan. Bake for 35 minutes. Remove from the oven and set on a cake rack. Allow to cool completely before removing the cake from the pan. Serve with the strawberry sauce.

continues

STRAWBERRY SAUCE

MAKES APPROXIMATELY 2 CUPS

You may wish to substitute other types of preserves for the strawberry.

One 8-ounce jar strawberry preserves
1 tablespoon potato starch
2 tablespoons dry red wine
1/2 cup pineapple preserves
1/2 pint fresh strawberries, thinly sliced
1 cup toasted almonds, chopped, for garnish
  (optional) (see Dad's Compote de Fruta Seca,
  page 54, to toast almonds)

1. Place the strawberry preserves in a small saucepan. In a 1-cup measure, mix the potato starch and wine together and add to the preserves. Heat the mixture over medium-high heat only until it begins to boil. Reduce to low and stir until thickened. Remove from the heat.

2. Fold in the pineapple preserves and fresh strawberries. Pour a little of the sauce, warm or at room temperature, over the cake. Sprinkle with almonds if desired. The sauce can be prepared several days ahead, refrigerated, and brought to room temperature before serving.

Matzo Products

Matzos

One 1³/4-ounce box soup nuts (*mandlen*)

Matzo cake meal

Dairy and Eggs

4 ounces margarine

1 dozen large eggs

4 ounces egg substitute

1 quart liquid nondairy creamer

Packaged Goods

One 8.9-ounce box Manischewitz angel food cake mix

One 7-ounce box egg drop soup mix

One 19-ounce jar duck sauce

Fish, Meat, and Poultry

4 ounces fresh whitefish fillets

4 ounces fresh carp fillets

One 24-ounce jar gefilte fish

2¹/2 to 3 pounds fresh or frozen boneless, skinless chicken breasts (4 whole breasts)

Vegetables

2 medium carrots

2 medium onions

One 17-ounce can sweet potatoes

Fruit and Nuts

4 medium lemons

¹/2 pint fresh strawberries

One 16-ounce can whole cranberry sauce

One 30-ounce can fruit cocktail

Two 20-ounce cans pineapple chunks

One 16-ounce can purple plums

One 16-ounce can mandarin orange segments

1 cup chopped almonds

Herbs, Spices, and Flavorings

Ground cardamom

Ground cinnamon

Ground cloves

Fresh mint leaves

Mild curry powder

Ground ginger

Black peppercorns

Salt and white pepper

Vanilla extract or vanilla sugar

Staples

One 8-ounce jar each apricot, pineapple, and strawberry preserves

Honey

Potato starch

Sugar

Brown sugar

Vegetable oil

Cooking spray

Beverages, Wine, and Spirits

2 ounces orange juice (optional)

Dry red wine

White wine

Table wine

Grape juice

Coffee, tea, and soft drinks

PREPARATION TIMETABLE

Things you can prepare a week or two ahead

Bake the chicken without the sauce, then freeze it.

Prepare the fruit compote. Cover and place in the refrigerator.

Two or three days before the Seder

Prepare the gefilte fish; cover and refrigerate.

Make the strawberry sauce; cover and refrigerate.

Cook the sweet and sour sauce; cover and refrigerate.

One day before the Seder

Bake the cake. Let cool, then cover well with plastic wrap.

Place the frozen chicken in the refrigerator to thaw.

On the day of the Seder

Bake the sweet potato timbale and prepare the cranberry puree. Refrigerate each separately, well covered.

Warm the sweet and sour sauce and pour over the chicken. Refrigerate until ready to warm the chicken.

Three hours before your Seder ceremony begins

Get the chicken soup ready for cooking.

Place the chicken in a 200°F oven to warm.

One hour before serving the festive meal

Warm the fruit compote or allow it to come to room temperature.

Place the sweet potato timbale and cranberry puree in a low oven to warm.

Place the gefilte fish on serving plates.

Prepare the beverages.

Just before you sit down to begin the festive meal

Bring the strawberry sauce to room temperature.

Finish the chicken soup.

Remove the timbale from the casserole to an ovenproof serving platter. Pour half of the cranberry puree over it and return to the oven to keep warm.

A Healthful Seder

And this day shall be unto you for a

memorial, and ye shall keep it a feast to the

Lord throughout your generations; ye shall

keep it a feast by an ordinanace forever.

—Exodus 12:14

There was a time when the answer to the question "What's for dinner?" was meat, potatoes, and apple pie with ice cream. No one counted calories, watched fat intake or cholesterol, or read food labels. Today we've become aware that a healthy mind and body comes from what we eat.

My friend Pat Streicher, a registered dietitian with the Cincinnati Cholesterol Center, helped create this menu. She says, "You want to enjoy yourself when special celebrations come along, so you can fudge a little." This Passover menu is truly something to celebrate, since it is low in fat and cholesterol, although not as low as your everyday meals may need to be.

CEREMONIAL FOODS FOR THE SEDER PLATE

(See chapter 3 for menu and recipes.)

FESTIVE MEAL MENU

Appetizer
Deviled "Egg" Pâté

First Course
Vegetable Broth with Matzo Balls

Salad
Mesclun Salad with Balsamic Vinaigrette
and Toasted Farfel

Entrée
Chicken Breasts, Well Preserved

Side Dishes
Shiitake Mushroom–Bell Pepper Matzo Kugel

Dessert
De-Light-Ful Sponge Cake

A Mélange of Berries

Beverages
Coffee, tea, and soft drinks

Suggested Wines
Kedem Sparkling Nonalcoholic
Grape Juice: Catawba or Peach
(appetizer)

Château De La Grave White Bordeaux
(first course and salad)

Baron Herzog Sauvignon Blanc
or Weinstock Chardonnay
(entrée)

Kedem Peach Grape Juice
(dessert)

DEVILED "EGG" PÂTÉ

MAKES 2 CUPS

It's wonderful what you can accomplish using egg substitutes. With Pat's help, I even learned how to hard-boil them. You may wish to double this recipe.

1 cup egg substitute

1/3 cup margarine, melted

1 teaspoon white vinegar

1 teaspoon grated onion

1 teaspoon curry powder

1/8 teaspoon salt (optional)

2 hard-boiled large eggs, or 3 hard-boiled large egg whites

Lettuce leaves, washed and patted dry

1. To prepare the egg substitute, pour it into a medium nonstick skillet, cover, and cook over very low heat until just firm to the touch, about 15 minutes. Let cool. Remove from the pan and dice.

2. Combine the melted margarine, vinegar, onion, curry powder, and salt, if using, in a blender or processor. Blend on medium-high speed or pulse several times just until combined.

3. With the blender or processor running, add the cooked egg substitute and blend or process until smooth. Remove and set aside.

4. Cut the hard-boiled eggs or egg whites in half. Place in the blender or processor and finely chop. Remove and combine with the egg substitute mixture.

5. Oil a medium bowl. Press the egg mixture into it and smooth the top. Cover with plastic wrap and refrigerate for several hours or overnight. Line small plates with lettuce leaves and, using an ice-cream scoop, top with the pâté.

Per Serving	(1/4 cup)
Total Calories	120
Total Fat	9g
Cholesterol	53mg
Sodium	208mg

VEGETABLE BROTH WITH MATZO BALLS

I always try to have some of this broth in my freezer. You need not peel the vegetables; just make sure you scrub them well.

2 large russet potatoes, scrubbed but not peeled
1 rib celery
4 medium carrots, sliced
2 parsnips, sliced
3 onions, quartered
1/4 cup chopped fresh parsley
1 bay leaf
16 black peppercorns
1 teaspoon salt
10 cups water
Matzo Balls (see recipe, page 74)

1. Place all the ingredients in a large stockpot, cover, and bring to a boil over high heat. Reduce the heat and simmer for at least 2 hours or until potatoes are soft when pierced with the tip of a knife.

2. Strain the stock through a colander lined with cheesecloth. With the back of a tablespoon, or fork, press the liquid from the vegetables. Discard vegetables. Refrigerate for up to 4 days or freeze for up to 3 months. Serve warm with matzo balls.

Variation
Discard the bay leaf and peppercorns first and puree the vegetables in a blender or food processor. Add a cup of skim milk to the broth along with the pureed vegetables, and you have cream of vegetable soup.

Per Serving
Total Calories	93
Total Fat	0g
Cholesterol	0mg
Sodium	24mg

continues

MATZO BALLS

MAKES 8 MEDIUM MATZO BALLS

These matzo balls are made without egg yolks. The parsley and carrots add color and flavor. Should you wish to start from scratch, you'll need 2 tablespoons of matzo meal for each egg white.

One 2¼-ounce packet matzo ball mix
⅛ teaspoon ground cinnamon
4 large egg whites
2 tablespoons minced fresh parsley
1 small carrot, finely grated
2 tablespoons vegetable oil

1. Empty the matzo ball mix into a small bowl and add the cinnamon. In a medium bowl, beat the egg whites just until they hold soft peaks, then gently fold in the parsley, carrot, and oil.

2. Fold in the matzo ball mixture a little at a time. Refrigerate for at least 15 minutes.

3. Partially fill a large pot with water and bring to a boil over high heat. Remove the matzo ball mixture from the refrigerator. Wet your hands with cold water and form a small amount of the matzo mixture into a ball. Drop it into the boiling water. After all the matzo balls are in the water, stir once, then cover. Reduce the heat to low and simmer the matzo balls for 20 to 30 minutes or until firm but not hard. Remove with a slotted spoon and place the matzo balls in the vegetable broth. Refrigerate or freeze.

Per Serving	(1 matzo ball)
Total Calories	75
Total Fat	4g
Cholesterol	0mg
Sodium	31mg

MESCLUN SALAD WITH BALSAMIC VINAIGRETTE AND TOASTED FARFEL

MAKES 8 SERVINGS

I was introduced to mesclun salad while visiting our son Glenn in California. Basically, mesclun is a combination of baby and bitter lettuces combined with mild herbs.

For me, mesclun salad has turned into a passion. I'll never forget the look on my son's face when I walked into his apartment carrying enough salad greens for an army. "Mom," he said, "we're only three for dinner." When I returned home, I relied on the goodness of my caterer friends to obtain mesclun. Today it's in the produce section of my supermarket.

BALSAMIC VINAIGRETTE

2 tablespoons semidry red wine
1/2 cup balsamic vinegar
1/8 teaspoon salt
1/8 teaspoon freshly ground black pepper
1/4 teaspoon sugar
1/4 cup olive oil

MESCLUN SALAD

8 cups mesclun salad mix
1 medium red onion, thinly sliced
1 cup Toasted Farfel (see recipe, page 76)

1. Prepare the vinaigrette dressing. Using a wire whisk, mix the red wine, vinegar, salt, pepper, and sugar together in a medium container. Slowly add the olive oil in a steady stream, whisking until the dressing is well blended. Place in the bottom of a large salad bowl.

2. Add the mesclun mix to the bowl. Top with the sliced onion. Cover with paper towels or a dish towel and refrigerate.

3. To serve, toss the salad, arrange on salad plates, and top each serving with the toasted farfel.

Per Serving	(1 3/4 tablespoons vinaigrette)
Total calories	260
Total fat	7 g
Cholesterol	0 mg
Sodium	41 mg

continues

TOASTED FARFEL

MAKES APPROXIMATELY 1 CUP

These "Passover croutons" are not only a great addition to soups but also make an addictive "nosh."

1 cup farfel, or 2 to 3 matzos broken into small pieces

2 teaspoons olive oil

1/4 teaspoon cracked black pepper

2 teaspoons chopped fresh herbs, such as oregano, basil, garlic, or chives

Preheat the oven to 375°F. In a large bowl, mix all the ingredients together with a fork. Spread the mixture evenly in a shallow pan. Bake for 15 minutes, until golden in color, stirring with a wooden spoon every 10 minutes. Store in an airtight sealed bag or freeze until ready to use.

Per Serving	(2 tablespoons)
Total calories	50
Total fat	2 g
Cholesterol	0 mg
Sodium	0 mg

CHICKEN BREASTS, WELL PRESERVED

MAKES 8 SERVINGS

I had some wonderful leftover black cherry preserves that I didn't want to throw away, so I came up with this recipe. The chicken can be prepared ahead and frozen for up to 1 month. Thaw overnight in the refrigerator, then reheat, covered with aluminum foil, in a 300°F oven for 30 minutes.

2 1/2 to 3 pounds boneless, skinless chicken
    breasts (4 whole breasts)
1 cup matzo cake meal
1/4 teaspoon salt
Pinch of ground white pepper
6 tablespoons margarine
One 16-ounce jar preserves, such as
    black cherry, pineapple, or apricot
1/2 cup white wine

1. Preheat the oven to 350°F. Cut the chicken breasts in half. Place the matzo cake meal in a pie plate and stir in the salt and pepper. Coat each breast half with the mixture and arrange them in a greased 9×13-inch baking dish.

2. Melt the margarine in a medium saucepan. Add the preserves and white wine. Bring to a boil over high heat, stirring well with a wooden spoon. Pour over the chicken breast halves. Bake, uncovered, for 30 to 45 minutes or until slightly brown and crisp. Serve.

Per Serving
Total Calories   494
Total Fat   10g
Cholesterol   66mg
Sodium   249mg

Shiitake Mushroom–Bell Pepper Matzo Kugel

Makes 8 servings

The shiitake mushrooms and red bell pepper give this traditional kugel a new look and fabulous flavor. Your family and Seder guests will love it.

1 tablespoon vegetable oil

1 small onion, diced

1 leek, white part only, sliced

1 cup chopped shiitake mushrooms, stems removed

1 medium red bell pepper, seeded and diced

2 cups crushed matzo or farfel

1 1/2 cups low-fat chicken broth, warmed

2 large eggs plus 2 large egg whites

Freshly ground black pepper to taste

1/8 teaspoon salt

1. Preheat the oven to 375°F. Lightly grease a shallow 6-cup casserole.

2. In a medium skillet, heat the oil over medium-high heat. Add the onion and leek and cook the until limp, about 10 minutes. Add the mushrooms and bell pepper and cook 5 minutes more.

3. Place the matzo or farfel in a small bowl and cover with the chicken broth. Allow to stand for about 5 minutes. Empty into a strainer and press out as much liquid as possible.

4. In a large bowl, lightly beat the whole eggs and egg whites together. Add the cooked vegetables, matzo or farfel, pepper, and salt. Mix well. Transfer the kugel to the prepared casserole and bake for 35 to 40 minutes or until the top is brown and crisp and the kugel is set. Serve immediately.

Per Serving

Total Calories	149
Total Fat	3g
Cholesterol	53mg
Sodium	172mg

DE-LIGHT-FUL SPONGE CAKE

MAKES 10 TO 12 SERVINGS

Now you can have your cake and eat it too! This one is low in fat. The consistency is light, and the flavor is traditional.

2 large lemons
1/3 cup matzo cake meal
1/3 cup potato starch
8 large egg whites
6 large eggs, separated
1 heaping cup sugar

1. Preheat the oven to 325°F. Have ready a 10-inch ungreased tube pan. In a small bowl, grate the lemon zest and juice the lemons. Set aside. Sift the matzo cake meal and potato starch together. Set aside. Make sure the mixing bowls and beaters of your electric mixer are free from fat and extra clean. If possible, use a large standing electric mixer.

2. Place 10 egg whites in a large mixing bowl, and 4 egg whites plus 6 yolks in another bowl. Beat the 10 whites until soft peaks begin to form. Turn the speed to high and add the sugar gradually, no more than 1/4 cup at a time. Beat until stiff peaks form.

3. Turn the mixer speed to medium-low. Add the egg yolks, remaining whites, lemon zest, and lemon juice. Beat until well mixed, about 2 minutes. The mixture should be pale yellow in color and hold a good soft peak.

4. Turn the mixer to its lowest speed. Add the sifted cake meal and potato starch, beating only until the dry mixture disappears. Remove the bowl from the mixer.

5. Gently pass a rubber spatula through the batter to make sure the cake meal is evenly distributed. Pour the batter into the tube pan, smoothing it with a rubber spatula. Bake for 50 to 60 minutes in the center of the oven. Invert the tube pan over a rack or neck of a bottle and allow it to cool for 30 to 45 minutes, until the sides are just slightly warm to the touch.

6. Remove the tube pan from the bottle or rack. Run a knife around the outer and inner edges of the cake and invert it onto a cake plate. Serve.

Per Serving	(1/12 of the cake)
Total Calories	162
Total Fat	4g
Cholesterol	182mg
Sodium	86mg

Note: For tips to keep your sponge cake from falling, see page 35.

A Mélange of Berries

A perfect dessert when the first berries of the season appear. I like to add a few drops of rose water or almond flavoring to this if I have some on hand. Sometimes if my family doesn't eat this up quickly enough, I'll puree it in the food processor and use it as a sauce over ice cream or sponge cake.

1 quart fresh strawberries, sliced
1 pint fresh raspberries
1 pint fresh blueberries
1 cup Chardonnay
1 cup honey
1/4 teaspoon almond extract
1/2 teaspoon ground cardamom
Fresh mint leaves for garnish

1. Wash the berries, put them in a medium bowl, and refrigerate for at least 6 hours before serving. Using a large slotted spoon, turn the berries at least once.

2. Place the Chardonnay and honey in a 1-quart glass container. Microwave for 3 minutes on high or cook over medium-high heat until well heated, about 5 minutes.

3. Remove from the heat. Add the almond extract and cardamom. Allow the mixture to cool before pouring over the berries.

4. Transfer the berries to a chilled serving bowl. Pour the cooled liquid over them. Top the berries with the fresh mint and serve.

Per Serving	
Total Calories	206
Total Fat	1g
Cholesterol	0mg
Sodium	0mg

Matzo Products

Matzos

One 4^1/$_2$-ounce package matzo ball mix

Matzo cake meal

Farfel or crushed matzos

Dairy and Eggs

8 ounces margarine

25 large eggs

One 8-ounce carton egg substitute

Fish, Meat, and Poultry

2^1/$_2$ to 3 pounds boneless, skinless chicken breasts (4 whole breasts)

1^1/$_2$ cups low-fat chicken broth

Vegetables

1 bunch carrots

1 bunch celery

1 leek

1 head lettuce

8 cups mesclun salad mix

One 3- to 4-ounce container shiitake mushrooms

1 medium red onion

4 medium white onions

2 parsnips

2 large potatoes

1 medium red bell pepper

Fruits and Nuts

2 large lemons

1 pint fresh blueberries

1 pint fresh raspberries

1 quart fresh strawberries

Herbs, Spices, and Flavorings

Almond extract

Bay leaves

Ground cardamom

Ground cinnamon

Curry powder

1 bunch fresh mint

1 bunch fresh oregano, basil, *or* chives *or* 1 head garlic

1 large bunch parsley

White pepper

Black peppercorns

Salt

Staples

One 16-ounce jar preserves: black cherry, pineapple, or apricot

Honey

Olive oil

Potato starch

Sugar

Vegetable oil

Balsamic vinegar

White vinegar

Beverages, Wine, and Spirits

Chardonnay

Semidry red wine

White wine

Table wine

Grape juice

Coffee, tea, and soft drinks

PREPARATION TIMETABLE

Things you can prepare a week or two ahead

Cook the vegetable broth and place in the freezer.

Complete the matzo balls and freeze in the broth.

Bake the chicken breasts and place in the freezer.

Toast the farfel and place in an airtight container.

Two or three days before the Seder

Bake the matzo kugel, then let cool, cover, and refrigerate.

Make the vinaigrette dressing and store in an airtight jar.

Thaw baked chicken breasts in the refrigerator.

One day before the Seder

Make the egg pâté, then cover with plastic wrap and refrigerate.

Bake the sponge cake, let cool completely, and place on a serving platter. Cover well with plastic wrap.

Prepare the berries, place in an airtight container, and refrigerate.

On the day of the Seder

Thaw the soup and matzo balls in your microwave or place in a cooking pot and refrigerate until ready to warm them later.

Prepare the salad in its serving bowl as directed. Cover with plastic wrap and refrigerate.

Three hours before your Seder ceremony begins

Scoop the egg pâté onto individual plates, then refrigerate.

One hour before serving the festive meal

Preheat the oven to 200°F. Cover the chicken and the kugel with foil and place in the oven to warm.

Warm the soup with the matzo balls on top of the stove on the lowest setting or warm in the microwave just before serving.

Just before you sit down to begin the festive meal

Unwrap the sponge cake.

BETSY'S ROAST BRISKET OF BEEF
SERVED WITH BETSY'S CARROT PUDDING

Ecumenical Potluck Seder

ALLEGRIA COHEN'S CHIZU SALADA,
ALLEGRIA COHEN'S SPINACH SALAD, ROASTED AUBERGINE,
SEPHARDIC SALADE SHACKSHOOKA, AND ORIENTAL SALADA

Sephardic Seder

BAKED APRICOT-GINGER CHICKEN
WITH SWEET AND SOUR SAUCE SERVED WITH ORIENTAL SALADA

"Off-the-Shelf" Seder

LEMON ANGEL PIE

Ecumenical Potluck Seder

A Vegetarian Seder

For now the Winter is past,

The rains are over and gone.

The blossoms have appeared in the Land

The time of pruning has come;

The Song of the turtledove

Is heard in our land.

—Song of Songs 2:11–12

According to some traditions, Adam and Eve were vegetarians, eating only fruits and vegetables in the garden of Eden. After Noah and the flood, God gave permission for us to eat the flesh of the animals but not the blood.

Today, families are more aware of what they eat and are living healthier lifestyles. You may have noticed that many of your family members have chosen a vegetarian diet, no longer eating meat, fowl, or fish. I've created this Seder menu for those who adhere to a vegetarian diet and for those who are perhaps having vegetarian guests at their Seder.

CEREMONIAL FOODS FOR THE SEDER PLATE

(See chapter 3 for menu and recipes.)

FESTIVE MEAL MENU

Appetizer
Isa Bartalini's Eggplant Spread

Pâté à Choux for Passover
(Mini Matzo Puffs)

First Course
Janice Miller's Carrot Soup

Salad
Baby Lettuces with
Sherry Vinaigrette Dressing

Entrées
Wild Mushroom Ragout

Sophie's Vegetables Extraordinaire

Desserts
Red Raspberry Sorbet

Brown Sugar Meringue Crisps

No-Yolk Chocolate Fudge Cake

Beverages
Coffee, tea, and soft drinks

Suggested Wines
Barentura Soave or Gamla Emerald Hill Red
(appetizer)

Baron Herzog Blush Muscat
(first course and salad)

Kedem Estate Red
(entrée)

Barbenura Asti Spumante
(dessert)

ISA BARTALINI'S EGGPLANT SPREAD

MAKES APPROXIMATELY 1 CUP

I met Isa while visiting Italy with my Russian cousin, Anna Popova, who was working on a picture for the Mosc Film Company. We had the pleasure of staying in Isa's home. This quick appetizer became a favorite. It keeps for up to a week in the refrigerator.

1 eggplant (approximately 1 pound)
Pinch of salt
1 small clove garlic
1/2 cup chopped fresh parsley
2 fresh bay leaves, or 1 teaspoon dried basil
1/2 cup plain low-fat yogurt
Olive oil

1. Preheat the oven to 325°F. Puncture the outside skin of the eggplant with the tip of a sharp knife in several places and bake it for 1 to 1 1/2 hours, or cook the eggplant in the microwave on high for 3 to 4 minutes on each side. Remove from the oven or microwave and allow the eggplant to cool for 5 to 10 minutes.

2. Slice the eggplant in half and remove the pulp. Place the pulp in a blender or food processor. Add the salt, garlic, parsley, and bay leaves or dried basil. Pulse several times, scraping the sides of the blender or food processor. The eggplant should be a little chunky. Process or blend 5 seconds more.

3. Remove the eggplant to a small bowl and fold in the yogurt. Serve with mini matzo crackers or mini matzo puffs (see recipe next page). Drizzle a little olive oil over the top of the spread. Cover and refrigerate.

PÂTÉ À CHOUX FOR PASSOVER

(MINI MATZO PUFFS)

MAKES 3¹/₂ TO 4 DOZEN MINI MATZO PUFFS

I adapted these Passover mini puffs from a recipe I learned in a cooking class taught by Marilyn Harris, my friend and a well-known Cincinnati culinary expert. Filled with mushrooms or cheese, these puffs make a great appetizer on their own. Sometimes I serve them plain with soup.

¹/₂ cup matzo cake meal
¹/₂ cup potato starch
Salt and ground white pepper to taste
6 tablespoons margarine, cut into pieces
1 cup water
4 extra-large eggs

1. Preheat the oven to 425°F. Grease a cookie sheet. In a bowl, sift the cake meal, potato starch, salt, and pepper together and set aside.

2. Bring the margarine and water to a boil over high heat. Remove the pan from the heat and add the sifted dry ingredients all at once. Beat well with a wooden spoon. Place back on heat for 1 to 2 minutes and keep stirring to extract all the moisture. Allow to cool for 10 to 15 minutes.

3. Place the matzo meal mixture in a food processor. With the machine running, add the eggs through the feed tube. Process until a ball begins to form. Remove dough to a pastry bag.

4. Using a pastry bag fitted with a straight decorating tube or your oiled hands, form the dough into small mounds or balls. Place them about 1¹/₂ inches apart on the prepared cookie sheet. Bake for 20 minutes. Remove and turn off the oven.

5. Pierce each puff on one side with the point of a knife. Return to the turned-off oven for 10 more minutes. Let cool, then split and fill or enjoy plain.

Variation
For larger dessert puffs, eliminate the salt and pepper and add 2 tablespoons sugar and 1 teaspoon vanilla or ¹/₄ teaspoon almond extract to the dough recipe. Make the puffs approximately 3 inches in diameter. Fill with ice cream, flavored whipped cream, or custard.

JANICE MILLER'S CARROT SOUP

MAKES 8 TO 10 SERVINGS

Janice was a member of my focus group for this cookbook, and her input and opinions were invaluable. Known for her entertaining expertise and fabulous meals, she stresses the importance of using butter for the right flavor.

4 ounces (1 stick) unsalted butter

6 cups coarsely grated carrots
   (about 2 pounds)

2 large cloves garlic, sliced

4 shallots, sliced

4 teaspoons fresh thyme leaves, or
   2 teaspoons dried thyme

2 large baking potatoes, peeled and cut
   into eighths

2 tablespoons pareve chicken soup
   granules

6 cups water

1 tablespoon freshly squeezed lemon juice

1 cup half-and-half or heavy cream

Salt and freshly ground black pepper
   to taste

1. Melt the butter in the bottom of a large stockpot over medium-low heat. Add the grated carrots and cook over medium-low heat for 20 to 25 minutes, stirring with a wooden spoon now and then, until the carrots turn a light orange color. Be sure the carrots do not brown.

2. Add the garlic and shallots. Cook 3 to 5 minutes more. Add the thyme, potatoes, instant soup granules, and water. Cover and bring to a boil over high heat. Reduce the heat to a simmer and cook for 30 minutes or until the vegetables are soft. Remove from the heat and allow the soup to rest, uncovered, for 15 to 20 minutes.

3. Strain the liquid from the vegetables into a large bowl. Puree the vegetables in batches using a food processor, food mill, or blender. Return the pureed vegetables and liquid to the soup pot. Add the lemon juice. Add the half-and-half or cream and season with salt and freshly ground pepper to taste. If the soup looks too thick, add a little more water.

BABY LETTUCES WITH
SHERRY VINAIGRETTE DRESSING

MAKES 1 CUP

Select different baby lettuces or purchase a pre-mixed package and toss with this vinaigrette dressing.

SHERRY VINAIGRETTE DRESSING

1/2 cup olive oil

1/2 teaspoon balsamic vinegar

2 tablespoons sherry

1 tablespoon freshly squeezed lemon juice

Salt and freshly ground black pepper
   to taste

SALAD

8 cups mixed baby lettuces

In a 2-cup measure, mix all the dressing ingredients together with a wire whisk until well blended. Toss with the lettuces in a large salad bowl.

WILD MUSHROOM RAGOUT

With the variety of mushrooms available at the supermarket today, this vegetarian entrée will elicit rave reviews from your guests. It's important to buy the freshest mushrooms. Don't let the number of ingredients scare you off. This is really easy to prepare.

1 tablespoon olive oil

3 cloves garlic, minced

1 medium onion, finely chopped

1 tablespoon finely chopped fresh sage

2 tablespoons finely chopped fresh
    winter savory

4 ounces white button mushrooms, trimmed
    and thinly sliced

8 ounces porcini mushrooms, trimmed
    and thinly sliced

8 ounces shiitake mushrooms, stems
    removed and thinly sliced

3 tablespoons soy sauce

1 cup Cabernet Sauvignon

2 tablespoons balsamic vinegar

4 teaspoons potato starch dissolved in
    1/2 cup cold water

Salt and freshly ground black pepper
    to taste

1 tablespoon minced fresh parsley for
    garnish

1. In a large, heavy skillet, heat the oil over medium heat. Add the garlic and cook, stirring, until pale golden in color, about 2 minutes. Add the onion, sage, and savory, stirring with a wooden spoon until the onion has softened, about 3 minutes.

2. Add all the mushrooms and the soy sauce to the skillet. Continue stirring until the liquid from the mushrooms cooks off and the mushrooms begin to brown, 5 to 10 minutes. Add the wine and vinegar; let everything come to a boil over high heat. Boil for 3 minutes, then add the potato starch mixture. Continue boiling 1 to 2 more minutes, stirring continuously.

3. Reduce the heat to low and simmer until the liquid just begins to thicken. Add salt and pepper to taste. Serve over rice for a Sephardic menu or noodles if serving an Ashkenazic menu. Garnish with parsley.

SOPHIE'S VEGETABLES EXTRAORDINAIRE

MAKES 6 SERVINGS

Sophie Bass is the aunt of Ilene Ross, who was in my cookbook focus group. Everyone loves this easy but elegant side dish, which Sophie prepares for most special family occasions. It's a good make-ahead dish. The sauce and vegetables are prepared separately. (For a fancier vegetable dish, you may want to try Lesha's Three-Vegetable Gateau, page 166.)

VEGETABLES

1 pound whole cauliflower, broken into florets

1 pound broccoli, cut into serving-size pieces

1 pound carrots, sliced into rounds

1 pound asparagus, stems peeled, or
   (if Sephardic) 1 pound green beans

SAUCE

1¹/₂ sticks butter or margarine

3 cloves garlic, minced

¹/₂ cup finely chopped fresh parsley

8 ounces mushrooms, thinly sliced

1. Cook or steam each vegetable separately in a large pot with water for 3 to 4 minutes or until crisp-tender.

2. Meanwhile, make the sauce. In a medium skillet, melt the butter or margarine over medium-low heat. Add the garlic and parsley and cook, stirring, for 5 minutes. Add the mushrooms, and cook for 10 to 15 minutes.

3. Lay the vegetables lengthwise side by side in a 9×13-inch casserole. Pour the sauce evenly over the top of the vegetables. Cover with aluminum foil and refrigerate.

4. To serve, preheat the oven to 275°F and warm the casserole in the oven for 15 minutes or until heated through.

RED RASPBERRY SORBET

Refreshing is the word for this sorbet. It can be made ahead and kept in your freezer until ready to serve.

2/3 cup water

2/3 cup sugar

1 tablespoon grated orange zest

One 10-ounce package frozen raspberries

1/2 cup bottled red raspberry syrup

1 pint fresh strawberries, sliced

1 cup heavy cream

1. To make a sugar syrup, combine the water and sugar in a 1-quart saucepan. Cook over medium-high heat, stirring constantly with a wooden spoon, until the sugar melts and you have a thick syrup. If you're using a microwave oven, place the water and sugar in a 4-cup glass measure and microwave on high for 3 to 5 minutes. Set aside to cool.

2. Place the orange zest, raspberries, red raspberry syrup, and strawberries in a food processor or blender and process for 15 seconds. With the machine running, pour the cooled sugar syrup through the opening. Process or blend 5 more seconds.

3. Empty the mixture into a medium metal bowl and cover with plastic wrap. Freeze for 2 to 4 hours or overnight.

4. Several hours before serving, remove the sorbet from the freezer. Loosen the sorbet from the metal bowl with the tip of a knife and cut into several pieces. Place the pieces in the processor or blender and pulse several times or until smooth. Add the heavy cream and process or blend until light and fluffy, 10 to 15 seconds. Empty the sorbet back into a clean metal bowl or freezer container. Cover well with plastic wrap and keep in the freezer until ready to serve.

BROWN SUGAR MERINGUE CRISPS

Marlene Sorosky's article on Passover desserts, published in the April 1995 issue of *Bon Appétit*, inspired me to create these light and delicious cookies. Soaking the raisins for 5 or 10 minutes in hot or boiling water allows the raisins to become soft and full, or "plumped." These cookies freeze well. If you don't intend to freeze them, store them in an airtight container.

4 large egg whites

1/4 teaspoon salt

*1 1/2 teaspoons vanilla extract, or
    2 teaspoons vanilla sugar*

1 1/2 cups firmly packed dark brown sugar

1 cup chopped pecans

1 tablespoon potato starch

*1 tablespoon matzo meal (not matzo
    cake meal)*

1/2 cup dark raisins, plumped (see headnote)

1. Preheat the oven to 400°F. Line 2 cookie sheets with aluminum foil.

2. In the large bowl of an electric mixer, beat the egg whites with the salt and vanilla or vanilla sugar on high speed just until they hold soft peaks. Gradually add the brown sugar, beating the meringue until it holds stiff peaks, 3 to 5 minutes total. The stiffer the meringue, the less it will spread during baking.

3. Spread the pecans out on a jelly roll pan or cookie sheet and toast in the oven for about 8 minutes or until golden brown. Set aside. Lower the oven temperature to 300°F.

4. In a small bowl, sift the potato starch and matzo meal together and sprinkle it over the meringue, along with the pecans and raisins. Combine everything on low speed no more than 3 seconds, or fold together with a spatula.

5. Drop the meringue by heaping teaspoons about 1 1/2 inches apart on the prepared baking sheets, forming 2-inch mounds. Bake in the middle of the oven no longer than 15 minutes or until they look firm on top. Turn the oven off and allow the cookies to remain in oven 15 more minutes.

6. Remove the baking sheets from the oven. Slide the foil with the cookies from the baking sheets onto a wire rack. Let the cookies cool on the foil for 5 minutes, then carefully peel the cookies off the foil and let them finish cooling on the rack. The cookies will be crisp on top and soft inside.

No-Yolk Chocolate Fudge Cake

Makes 8 to 12 servings

High in flavor, low in cholesterol, this rich, dense cake may fall a little as it cools. It's best to prepare the cake 2 to 3 days ahead, and then refrigerate it. Finish glazing it on the day you serve it.

CAKE

2/3 cup walnut halves, toasted and cooled (see
    La Salada Vert, page 53, to toast walnuts)

1/2 cup unsweetened cocoa powder

1 tablespoon grated orange zest

1 1/2 cups sugar, divided

1 tablespoon freshly squeezed orange juice

7 large egg whites

1/4 teaspoon salt

1/4 cup unsalted margarine, melted and cooled

GLAZE AND GARNISH

2/3 cup chopped semisweet good-quality chocolate

1 1/2 tablespoons freshly squeezed orange juice

3 tablespoons unsalted margarine

1 tablespoon sugar

Pinch of salt

6 walnut halves

Making the Cake

1. Preheat the oven to 350°F. Grease an 8-inch springform pan. Place the walnuts in a food processor or blender and pulse several times. Add the cocoa powder, orange zest, and 3/4 cup of the sugar; process

or blend until finely ground. Be careful not to grind this to a paste. Stir in the orange juice and set aside.

2. In the large bowl of an electric mixer, beat the egg whites with the salt until they begin to hold soft peaks; gradually add the remaining 3/4 cup sugar, about 2 tablespoons at a time, beating after each addition, until the egg whites begin to hold stiff peaks. Do not beat too stiff.

3. Gently stir about 1/3 of the egg whites into the walnut mixture. Fold in the remaining egg whites. Add the cooled margarine and fold everything together gently but thoroughly.

4. Pour the batter into the prepared pan. Bake in the middle of the oven for 40 minutes or until a tester inserted in the middle of the cake comes out clean. Remove the cake and let it cool completely in the pan on a rack. Run a knife around the edge of the cake and remove the sides of the pan. Tightly wrap the cake and refrigerate until ready to glaze.

Glazing the Cake

1. In a small heavy saucepan, combine the chocolate, orange juice, margarine, sugar, and salt. Stir over moderately low heat until the margarine is melted and smooth.

2. Carefully invert the cake onto a rack that has been set in a shallow baking pan. Pour the glaze over cake, tilting the cake if desired to allow the glaze to drip down the sides. Garnish with walnut halves, then chill, uncovered, for 30 to 45 minutes or until the glaze is set. Serve at room temperature.

Matzo Products
Matzos

Matzo cake meal

Matzo meal

Dairy and Eggs
8 ounces butter, unsalted

1 pound margarine

1/2 pint half-and-half

1 pint heavy cream

1/2 dozen extra-large eggs

1 dozen large eggs

One 8-ounce carton plain low-fat yogurt

Vegetables
1 pound broccoli

3 pounds carrots

1 pound cauliflower

1 pound asparagus or green beans

1 eggplant

1 pound white button mushrooms

8 ounces porcini mushrooms

Baby lettuce

8 ounces shiitake mushrooms

1 medium onion

2 large baking potatoes

4 shallots

Fruits and Nuts
One 10-ounce package frozen raspberries

1 pint fresh strawberries

1/2 cup dark raisins

1 lemon

1 orange

1 cup pecans

1 cup walnuts

Herbs, Spices, and Flavorings
Bay leaves or dried basil

Pareve chicken soup granules

1 head garlic

1 bunch fresh parsley

Fresh sage leaves

Soy sauce

Fresh or dried thyme

Vanilla extract or vanilla sugar

Fresh winter savory

Black peppercorns

Ground white pepper

Salt

Red raspberry syrup

Staples
Semisweet chocolate

Cocoa powder, unsweetened

Olive oil

Potato starch

Sugar

Brown sugar

Balsamic vinegar

Rice or Passover noodles

Beverages, Wine, and Spirits
Orange juice

Cabernet Sauvignon

Sherry

Table wine

Grape juice

Coffee, tea, and soft drinks

PREPARATION TIMETABLE

Things you can prepare a week or two ahead

Make the carrot soup and freeze until the day of the Seder.

Make sorbet and freeze until just before serving.

Two or three days before the Seder

Prepare the eggplant spread; cover and refrigerate.

Mix the vinaigrette dressing and refrigerate in a covered container.

Bake the chocolate fudge cake.

Make the mushroom ragout; cover and refrigerate.

Cook vegetables for Sophie's Vegetables Extraordinaire.

Make the brown sugar meringue crisps and store.

One day before the Seder

Bake the mini puffs, let cool completely, and store in an airtight container.

On the day of the Seder

Complete the salad, cover with a dish towel, and refrigerate.

Thaw the carrot soup.

Make sauce for Sophie's Vegetables Extraordinaire. Cool and refrigerate.

Glaze the chocolate fudge cake. Chill, uncovered.

Three hours before your Seder ceremony begins

Place the eggplant on individual serving plates; cover and refrigerate.

Place the mini puffs in a serving basket.

One hour before serving the festive meal

Add sauce to Sophie's Vegetables Extraordinaire. Cover and warm in a 275°F oven.

Warm the mushroom ragout, covered, in a 275°F oven.

Just before you sit down to begin the festive meal

Warm the soup over low heat.

Arrange the meringue crisps on a serving plate.

Move the sorbet from the freezer to the refrigerator.

AN ECUMENICAL POTLUCK SEDER

For the acts of kindness God showed
our people we say Dayenu *(Die-ay-new).*
That alone would have been enough,
for that alone we are grateful.

—Haggadah

This potluck menu contains dairy, meat, and pareve recipes. Those following the kosher dietary laws may wish to eliminate some recipes or substitute others. I have developed a key for this menu: M for meat recipes, D for dairy recipes, and P for pareve, or neutral, recipes.

For twenty-four years a group of friends, both Christians and Jews, have held a yearly Passover Seder. The host is Jewish, but there is representation from a spectrum of committed Christians, nonobservant Jews, practicing Jews, and even some agnostics. Several of the recipes come from my family's traditional celebrations and have become standard fare on the menu.

My long-time Cincinnati friend Melissa Lanier was kind enough to send me the complete menu and recipes. "Over the years," she told me, "this celebration has come to mean a great deal to all of us and has hopefully made us all the more respectful of different religious traditions. Though the menu is potluck, were someone to substitute for a much-loved dish some new stylish version, there is the risk that they would be roundly criticized because this potluck menu is predetermined and anticipated with relish."

CEREMONIAL FOODS FOR THE SEDER PLATE

(See chapter 3 for menu and recipes.)

FESTIVE MEAL MENU

First Course
Grandmother Jacob's Chicken Soup
with Matzo Balls (M)
(See page 29 for the recipe.)

Entrées
The Turkey's in the Bag (M)

Betsy's Roast Brisket of Beef (M)

Side Dishes
Betsy's Carrot Pudding (P)

Judge George Palmer's Company
Cauliflower (D)

Jane Palmer's Mushrooms Florentine (D)

Desserts
Dena's Chocolate Mousse Torte
from Israel (P)

Lemon Angel Pie (P)

Fresh Fruit Salad (P)

Beverages
Coffee, tea, and soft drinks

Suggested Wines
Herzog De La Grave Red
or Weinstock Cabernet Sauvignon
(entrée)

Gamla Rose of Cabernet
(dessert)

THE TURKEY'S IN THE BAG (M)

MAKES 10 TO 12 SERVINGS

I've selected a recipe I prepare for my family on Thanksgiving. For those who insist on a traditional roasting method, check out my "Turkey Tips" and suggested roasting times for roasting your turkey the old-fashioned way—without a cooking bag.

2 tablespoons matzo cake meal

1 turkey-size cooking bag (19 by 23 1/2 inches)

One 12- to 16-pound turkey, at room temperature

1 navel orange with peel, sliced

1 large onion, quartered

1 McIntosh apple, quartered

6 dried apricots

Juice and grated zest of 1 orange

1/2 cup apricot preserves

1. Preheat the oven to 350°F. Place the cake meal in the cooking bag and shake the bag so the cake meal is evenly distributed. Place the bag in a large roasting pan at least 2 inches deep. Remove the giblets from the turkey and discard. Rinse the turkey inside and out with cold water, drain, and dry it well with paper towels.

2. Place the orange slices, onion and apple quarters, and dried apricots in the turkey cavity. Secure the neck skin with a metal skewer. Tuck the drumsticks under a band of skin or tie together with string.

TIPS FOR ROASTING THE OLD-FASHIONED WAY

- Turkeys are not uniformly sized—use a roasting chart as a guide.

- Allow 1/2 to 1 pound for each serving.

- Roast your turkey on a rack in an open pan.

- Choose a roasting pan large enough to hold your turkey.

- If the turkey is stuffed, add 30 minutes to the cooking time for smaller turkeys and up to 60 minutes for larger ones.

- Make sure your oven will accommodate the girth of the turkey. You may need to use 2 small birds.

- If using a foil roasting pan, double it for extra strength.

3. In a 2-cup measure, mix the orange juice and zest with the apricot preserves. Rub the outside of the turkey with this glaze.

4. Place the turkey in the cooking bag, breast side up. Close the bag with the tie provided and make six 1/2-inch slits in the top of the bag with the tip of a sharp knife. If using a meat thermometer, insert it through a slit in the bag, into the center of a thigh, next to the body. Be sure the thermometer does not touch the bone.

5. Roast for 2 hours to 2 hours 45 minutes or until the thermometer registers 180°F. Remove the turkey from the oven and allow it to stand (in the cooking bag) for 15 minutes. If the turkey sticks to the bag, gently loosen it before opening the bag.

6. To open, keep the bag and turkey in the baking pan. Carefully cut or slit the top of the bag and remove the turkey. Take the fruit and onion from inside the cavity and discard them. Allow the turkey to rest for 20 to 30 minutes before carving.

Note: If you're feeding a small number of people, a turkey breast can be used instead of the whole turkey. Lay the orange, apricots, apple, and onion under the breast and use a smaller baking bag. Roast the turkey breast according to its weight.

Roasting Chart

To make sure the thighs are well roasted, cut and check the bird at the hip joints. If you see that the turkey is not cooked enough for your liking, raise the oven heat but be sure to protect the breast from getting too brown by covering it with aluminum foil, shiny side up.

Weight with giblets	Temperature	Time Unstuffed
10–12 pounds	350°F	1 1/2–2 1/4 hours
14–20 pounds	325°F	2–3 hours
24–28 pounds	325°F	3 1/2–4 hours

BETSY'S ROAST BRISKET OF BEEF (M)

Paul and Betsy Sittenfeld's Cincinnati home is well known for hospitality. The potluck Seder has been held in their home since its inception.

Brisket is a favorite entrée in my home also. Because it's a grainy cut of the forequarter, it needs to be simmered slowly for several hours. It is best prepared several days ahead, then refrigerated. That way the fat will congeal and become easy to remove. This brisket freezes well.

One 4-pound whole beef brisket
1¹/₂ teaspoons salt
Freshly ground black pepper to taste
1 tablespoon vegetable oil
3 large onions, sliced
2 cloves garlic, peeled
2 whole bay leaves
¹/₂ cup ketchup
¹/₂ cup cold water
1 tablespoon potato starch

1. Preheat the oven to 375°F. Rinse the brisket in cold water and dry with paper towels. Rub the brisket all over with the salt and pepper. Spread the oil in a large Dutch oven. Place the brisket, fat side up, in the pan. Brown it in the oven without searing, 20 to 30 minutes.

2. Remove the pan from the oven. Surround the brisket with the onions and garlic. Cover with the bay leaves, ketchup, and cold water.

3. Lower the oven temperature to 325°F. Cover the pan with a lid and roast the brisket for about 3 hours, basting now and then. The brisket should be tender but not too soft. To test for doneness, stick a fork into the flat, leaner end of the brisket. There should be a little resistance when the fork is pulled out. This is what is known as fork-tender.

4. Remove the brisket from the oven. Separate the brisket from the liquid and vegetables. If serving immediately, allow the brisket to cool for 30 minutes before slicing. Otherwise, refrigerate the brisket, well covered.

5. The liquid and vegetables remaining in the pan make a great gravy. Place the liquid and vegetables in a blender or food processor along with 1 tablespoon potato starch. Pulse several times, then process for 10 seconds or until smooth. Empty the gravy into a 4-cup container and refrigerate.

6. When ready to serve, remove any congealed fat from the brisket. Using a sharp knife, slice the brisket against the grain, or muscle lines. Place the slices in a casserole. Remove any solidified fat from the gravy and pour the gravy over the brisket. Warm in a 300°F oven for about 30 minutes before serving.

BETSY'S CARROT PUDDING (P)

MAKES 8 SERVINGS

Betsy prepares this recipe 2 or 3 days ahead. One hour before serving, she covers it with aluminum foil and warms it in a 200°F degree oven. She never serves this piping hot, only warmed.

3 cups thinly sliced carrots

1 bay leaf

1 medium onion, quartered

1/4 teaspoon salt

1 tablespoon ground cinnamon

Pinch of ground nutmeg

1 tablespoon ground ginger

5 large eggs, separated

3/4 cup sugar

1/2 cup matzo meal

1 cup chopped walnuts

1. Place the carrots in a large saucepan with just enough water to cover them. Add the bay leaf, onion, and salt. Cover and bring to a boil. Reduce the heat and simmer until tender, 15 to 20 minutes. Remove the bay leaf and onion and drain the carrots.

2. Mash the carrots with a potato masher or in your food processor. Stir in the cinnamon, nutmeg, and ginger. Pulse 2 to 3 times or beat with a wire whisk until smooth. Remove to a large bowl and set aside.

3. In a large bowl, beat the egg yolks and sugar with a wire whisk. Add to the carrots. With an electric mixer, beat the egg whites until stiff. Fold them into the carrot mixture along with the matzo meal. Add the nuts and mix everything well.

4. Preheat the oven to 350°F. Butter a 9×13-inch shallow baking dish. Pour the carrot mixture into the prepared baking dish and bake for 40 minutes or just until firm.

JUDGE GEORGE PALMER'S
COMPANY CAULIFLOWER (D)

MAKES 6 SERVINGS

After looking at the ingredients in this recipe, I realized how it got its name. The flavor is rich and delicious. The consistency, wonderfully creamy. Don't count the calories! Just enjoy—it's a holiday!

If you are following the kosher dietary laws and your main entrée is meat, you may want to substitute another side dish.

1 medium head cauliflower
Salt and freshly ground black pepper
   to taste
1/2 cup sour cream
1/2 cup shredded sharp cheddar cheese
1 teaspoon toasted sesame seeds

1. Break the cauliflower into florets and place in a large saucepan. Add a small amount of boiling water. Cover and cook over medium heat until tender, 10 to 15 minutes. Drain well.

2. Preheat the oven to 350°F. Place the cauliflower in a 1-quart casserole; season with salt and pepper. Spread the sour cream evenly over the top of the cauliflower. Sprinkle with the cheese. Top with the sesame seeds. (You can prepare the casserole up to this point, cover and refrigerate, and bake it right before serving.) Bake for 5 to 10 minutes or until the cheese melts and the sour cream is heated through. Serve warm.

Note: To toast sesame seeds, place in a small shallow pan. Place in a 300°F oven for about 5 minutes or until light golden in color.

JANE PALMER'S MUSHROOMS FLORENTINE (D)

MAKES 6 SERVINGS

The original recipe for this side dish came from the 1967 Cincinnati Civic Garden Center's cookbook. My testers adapted it just a little. This can be prepared in advance and refrigerated until time for baking.

Remember, this ecumenical Seder does not follow dietary law. If your main entrée is meat, you may wish to substitute another side dish or use margarine instead of butter and eliminate the cheese.

1 pound mushrooms, sliced

4 teaspoons melted butter

1/4 cup chopped onion

Two 10-ounce packages frozen chopped
    spinach, or 1 pound fresh spinach, cooked,
    drained, and chopped

1 clove garlic, finely minced

1 teaspoon salt

1 teaspoon ground nutmeg

1 cup grated sharp cheddar cheese

1. Preheat the oven to 350°F. Place 1 teaspoon of the melted butter in a medium skillet. Add the onions, and sauté over medium heat for 3 to 4 minutes. Add the mushrooms and sauté 5 more minutes. Set aside.

2. In a medium bowl, mix the cooked spinach with the garlic, salt, nutmeg, and remaining melted butter. Line a shallow 1 1/2-quart casserole with half the spinach mixture. Sprinkle with 1/3 cup of cheese and top with half the sautéed mushroom mixture. Repeat the layering, ending with the remaining cheese. Bake for 20 minutes or until the cheese is melted.

MAKES 10 TO 12 SERVINGS

Dena Jerimiahu, of blessed memory, and her husband, Joseph, lived in Cincinnati for a short time and then moved back to Israel. In 1975, when I went on my first United Jewish Appeal Mission to Israel, I visited her. She served this torte for dessert and shared the recipe with me. It has become a Passover favorite for many and a standard at the ecumenical Seder. If you use the heavy cream and butter instead of the pareve whipped topping and margarine, this torte becomes dairy.

TORTE

6 large eggs, separated

1 1/2 cups sugar

8 ounces margarine or unsalted butter (2 sticks), softened

8 ounces semisweet chocolate, melted and cooled (see Note)

1/2 cup ground almonds

1/4 cup brandy

1/4 cup matzo cake meal

WHIPPED TOPPING

One 8-ounce carton of pareve whipped topping or 1 cup heavy cream

1 1/2 tablespoons sugar (if using heavy cream only)

1/2 teaspoon vanilla extract or brandy

GARNISH

Grated chocolate or chocolate curls

1. Preheat the oven to 350°F. Grease a 9-inch springform pan. Line the bottom with waxed paper and grease it also.

2. Place the egg whites in a large mixing bowl and, using an electric mixer, beat on high speed until they begin to hold soft peaks. Add 1/2 cup of the sugar, 2 tablespoons at a time, until the whites hold stiff peaks but are not dry, about 5 minutes. Set aside.

3. In a large mixing bowl, beat the egg yolks until thick and lemony in color, 10 to 15 minutes. Add the softened margarine or butter, the remaining 1 cup sugar, and the cooled chocolate, beating at medium speed. Then beat on high speed for 2 minutes. Fold the reserved beaten egg whites into the chocolate mixture.

4. Fold the ground nuts, brandy, and cake meal into the chocolate batter. Pour into the prepared pan. Bake for 50 to 60 minutes or until a toothpick inserted into the center of the torte comes out almost clean. A crust will form on top while torte bakes.

5. Let the torte cool on a wire rack for 5 to 10 minutes before releasing the sides of the springform pan. Remove the sides and allow the torte to cool completely. It will fall a little in the center as it cools.

6. Invert the torte onto a serving platter and remove the waxed paper.

7. Prepare the whipped topping by pouring the pareve whipped topping or heavy cream into well-chilled bowl. Beat with chilled beaters until it starts to thicken, about 3 minutes. Add the sugar, if desired, and vanilla or brandy and beat until fairly stiff, 3 minutes more (or follow the directions on the pareve whipped topping container).

8. Frost the sides and top of the torte with the whipped topping. Garnish with grated chocolate or chocolate curls if desired. A portion of the whipped cream can be piped through a pastry bag to make it more decorative. For those who love a lot of whipped cream, the whipped cream recipe can be doubled.

Note: To microwave chocolate, place chocolate pieces in an uncovered microwave-safe bowl and microwave on high for 1 minute. Stir the chocolate. Microwave at additional 10- to 20-second intervals, stirring between intervals, until the chocolate is melted and smooth.

LEMON ANGEL PIE (P)

This delicious and different dessert, a standard at the Seder, has become a popular party dessert throughout the year. If you use the heavy cream and butter instead of the pareve whipped topping and margarine, this pie becomes dairy.

PIE SHELL

4 large egg whites

1 teaspoon white vinegar

1 teaspoon vanilla extract or inside scraped from 1 vanilla bean

1¹/₄ cups sugar

FILLING

1¹/₂ cups sugar

¹/₃ cup potato starch

¹/₈ teaspoon salt

2 cups water

6 egg yolks, slightly beaten

Grated zest of 1 lemon

¹/₂ cup freshly squeezed lemon juice

3 tablespoons margarine or butter

TOPPING

One 8-ounce carton pareve whipped topping, or 1 cup heavy cream, whipped

¹/₄ cup shredded coconut or ¹/₄ cup toasted almonds (see Dad's Compote de Fruta Seca, page 54, to toast almonds)

Making the Pie Shell

1. Preheat the oven to 200°F. With margarine or butter, grease a deep 10-inch glass pie plate well or the meringue crust will stick to the pie plate.

2. With an electric mixer, beat the egg whites at medium-high speed until they are frothy. Add the vinegar and vanilla. Turn the mixer speed to high. When the egg whites begin to hold soft peaks, start adding the sugar, 2 tablespoons at a time, beating thoroughly after each addition. Continue until all the sugar has been added and the egg whites are stiff and glossy but not too dry.

3. Spread the meringue in the well-greased pie plate, building up the sides and leaving the center flattened to hold the filling. Bake for 1 hour. Turn off the heat and allow the pie shell to remain in the oven for 1 hour with the door slightly ajar.

4. Remove the pie shell from the oven and let it cool completely. The center of the meringue crust may rise a little during baking and can be crushed to hold the filling after it has cooled. The crust can be prepared earlier in the day. Do not place in the refrigerator.

Making the Filling

1. In a large nonreactive saucepan, combine the sugar, potato starch, and salt. Gradually stir in the water. In a medium-sized bowl, mix the egg yolks, lemon zest, and lemon juice together. Slowly stir this mixture into the saucepan.

2. Over medium heat, using a wire whisk, cook the filling, stirring continuously, just until the mixture begins to thicken and become bubbly. Remove from the heat and stir in the margarine or butter. Allow the filling to cool for 15 to 20 minutes.

3. Meanwhile, make the topping. Preheat oven to 400°F. Spread the coconut on a cookie sheet. Bake 5 to 8 minutes until coconut turns light brown. Be sure to watch it carefully, as it browns quickly.

4. Fill the meringue shell. Place a layer of plastic wrap directly on top of the filling so it doesn't form a crust. When ready to serve, top with pareve whipped topping or whipped cream and garnish with toasted coconut or toasted almonds.

FRESH FRUIT SALAD (P)

This dessert is as simple as you can get. The combination of fruits you choose depends on what's in season. Sometimes I mix canned or frozen fruits with fresh fruit. One combination I like is canned pineapple with bananas, apples, oranges, and pears. Another is thawed frozen peaches with oranges, melon, bananas, and strawberries. Choose whatever fruits you enjoy, but remember, fruit needs to be sliced no more than 3 or 4 hours before serving to prevent discoloration.

3 to 4 pounds assorted fresh fruit, sliced

Sugar or honey to taste

2/3 cup orange juice

1 tablespoon orange liqueur (optional)

1/2 cup almonds, toasted and slivered, optional (see Dad's Compote de Fruta Seca, page 54, to toast almonds)

Cut the fruit into bite-size pieces. Place in a large bowl. Using a wire whisk, mix the sugar or honey with the orange juice and liqueur (if desired) in a small bowl. Gently pour over the prepared fruit. If using, fold in the almonds. Cover and refrigerate until ready to serve.

Matzo Products
Matzos

Matzo cake meal

Matzo meal

Dairy and Eggs
12 ounces butter or margarine

1 pound sharp cheddar cheese

1 pint heavy cream or two 8-ounce cartons pareve whipped topping

8 ounces sour cream

1 dozen large eggs

Fish, Meat, and Poultry
4-pound whole beef brisket

4- to 5-pound stewing chicken with giblets, cut up

12- to 16-pound turkey

Vegetables
1 large bunch carrots

1 medium head cauliflower

1 small bunch celery

1 pound mushrooms

5 large onions

2 medium onions

1 large parsnip

Two 10-ounce packages frozen spinach, or 1 pound fresh

Fruits and Nuts
1 McIntosh apple

4 ounces dried apricots

3 lemons

2 navel oranges

2/3 cup orange juice

3 to 4 pounds assorted fresh fruit for salad

1/2 cup ground almonds

1 cup slivered almonds (optional)

1 cup chopped walnuts

Shredded coconut

Herbs, Spices, and Flavorings
Bay leaves

Ground cinnamon

Whole cloves

1 head garlic

Ground ginger

Ketchup

Ground nutmeg

1 small bunch parsley

Freshly ground black pepper

Ground white pepper

Salt

Sesame seeds

Vanilla extract

Staples
Apricot preserves

1 pound semisweet chocolate

Honey

Potato starch

Sugar

Vegetable oil

White vinegar

Chocolate bar

Beverages, Wine, and Spirits
Brandy

Orange liqueur (optional)

Table wine

Grape juice

Coffee, tea, and soft drinks

PREPARATION TIMETABLE

If you're lucky, your guests will bring some of these recipes in the spirit of a potluck; however, if you find yourself tying on that apron, here's a timetable for preparing the dishes.

Things you can prepare a week or two ahead

Cook the soup and matzo balls, then freeze them. (See page 29 for the recipe.)

Roast the brisket, slice, and place in an ovenproof casserole with the gravy on top. Cover well and freeze.

Two or three days before the Seder

Make the carrot pudding, cover with plastic wrap, and refrigerate.

Thaw brisket and soup.

One day before the Seder

Cook the cauliflower. Assemble the casserole. Cover and refrigerate.

Sauté the mushrooms, cook the spinach, assemble the casserole, cover with plastic wrap, and refrigerate.

Bake the chocolate mousse torte; wrap well.

On the day of the Seder

Roast the turkey.

Finish the chocolate mousse torte with topping and garnish.

Make the lemon angel pie.

Three hours before your Seder ceremony begins

Fix the fruit salad.

Whip the pareve whipped topping or cream, place on top of the lemon angel pie, and refrigerate.

One hour before serving the festive meal

Preheat the oven to 275°F. Place the carrot pudding and brisket in the oven to warm.

Slice the turkey, place on an ovenproof platter, and warm in the oven, covered.

Just before you sit down to begin the festive meal

Warm the soup.

Bake mushroom Florentine.

Warm the cauliflower.

ADDITIONAL RECIPES
FOR PASSOVER

Cooking for Passover is always a challenge, especially cooking for the Seder. The recipes in this chapter provide choices for Seder menu substitutions and variety for those wishing to keep Passover for the remaining six or seven days. A large number of these recipes can be used for other celebrations and Jewish holidays throughout the year. See chapter 2 for information on recipe ingredients, food products, and beverages designated kosher for Passover.

Appetizers
Baked Cream Cheese Torte

Chopped Liver

Easy Chopped Herring*

Endive Nibblers*

Olive Spread*

Passover Pizza

Salmon Pâté

Sephardic Spiced Nuts*

Sylvia Rauchman's
Sweet-and-Sour Meatballs*

Soups
Blender Beet Borscht*

Cold Melon and Yogurt Soup

Cream of Tomato Soup*

Cucumber-Mint Soup*

Roasted Sweet Bell Pepper Soup

Egg Drop Soup

Sherried Mushroom Soup*

Vegetarian Borscht

Zucchini Bisque

Salads
Artichoke Antipasto Salad*

Carrot-Raisin Salad

Four Bell Pepper Salad

Ginger Chicken Salad

Herbed Potato Salad

Tuna Salad for Kids*

Warm Turkey Salad

Sauces
Easy Hollandaise

Fruit Tartar Sauce

Orange Sauce for Sponge Cake*

Schmaltz
(Rendered Chicken Fat)

Salsa for Kids*

Vanilla Sauce

Very Berry Sauce*

Entrées
Blintzes, Blintzes, and More Blintzes

Cabbage Rolls in Sweet-and-Sour Sauce

Glazed Salmon

Halibut Steaks in Foil

Lake Trout Baked in White Wine

Marilyn's Lean Lemon-Glazed
Meat Loaf

Hachis Parmentier*
(Moroccan Shepherd's Pie)

Ora's Brisket

Roast Lamb with Garlic Rosemary Sauce

Scalloped Orange Roughy

Stuffed Whitefish with White Wine

Scarlet Chicken

Turkey Scaloppini with Marinated Tomatoes

Vegetarian Roast

Vegetables and Side Dishes
Apple Matzo Kugel

Carrot-Yam Tzimmes*

Hanna Bear's Levivot
(Cauliflower Fritters)

Macaroni and Cheese Passover Style

Yelena Rura's Mushrooms Julienne

Rhubarb Compote

Ruth's Matzo Farfel Dressing

Lesha's Three-Vegetable Gateau

Spinach-Vegetable Squares

Tomato Slices Provençal*

Zucchini au Gratin

"Breads"
Assorted Muffins

Passover Banana "Bread"

Garlic "Bread"

Judy's Matzo Bagels

Onion Rolls for Passover

Desserts
Apples with Meringue Topping*

Apricot Freeze

Brandied Fresh Grapes*

Carrot Cake for Passover
with Cream Cheese Glaze

Cheesecake Extraordinaire*

Glazed Apple Tart

Frozen Amaretto Torte*

Passover Jelly Roll

Lemon Thins

Rocky Road Candy*

Watermelon Ice

Recipes designated with an asterisk(*) are "off-the-shelf" recipes that take advantage of packaged or frozen products.

BAKED CREAM CHEESE TORTE

MAKES 12 TO 16 SERVINGS

This appetizer brought rave reviews from both adults and children attending a family party I gave during Passover. Its savory flavor and smooth texture appealed to everyone.

Three 8-ounce packages low-fat cream cheese, softened

1 cup small-curd cottage cheese

2 cups low-fat sour cream

3 cloves garlic

2 tablespoons each chopped fresh oregano, basil, thyme, and chives

2 large eggs

2 large egg whites

2 tablespoons potato starch

1/2 teaspoon salt

1/4 teaspoon freshly ground black pepper

1/2 cup grated Parmesan cheese

Fresh chopped herbs

Sliced olives

Matzo crackers

1. Preheat the oven to 300°F. Grease a 9-inch springform pan.

2. Cut the cream cheese blocks in half. Place in the bowl of a food processor. (If you haven't got a processor with a 6- or 7-cup work bowl, make this in several batches.) Pulse several times. Add the cottage cheese and process for 30 seconds or until smooth, scraping down the sides as necessary. Add 1 1/3 cups of the sour cream and the garlic, oregano, basil, thyme, and chives and pulse 5 or 6 times or until combined.

3. Mix the eggs and egg whites together in a 2-cup measure. With the processor running, pour the eggs through the feed tube.

4. In a small bowl, mix the potato starch, salt, pepper, and Parmesan cheese. Add to the cheese mixture in the processor. Pulse 3 to 4 times, then process until smooth.

5. Pour the mixture into the prepared pan. Place on a cookie sheet in the lower third of the oven. Bake for 60 to 70 minutes or until the top just begins to brown. Turn off the oven, leaving the door ajar, and allow the cheese torte to remain in the oven for 30 minutes. The torte may fall in the middle at this point but it doesn't affect the end result. Remove from the oven and let cool on a wire rack. Cover and refrigerate overnight.

6. When ready to serve, remove the sides of the pan and, with a spatula, loosen the torte from the bottom. Slide onto a serving plate. Spread the remaining sour cream on top of the torte and garnish with fresh herbs or sliced olives. Accompany with assorted miniature matzo crackers.

CHOPPED LIVER

MAKES 6 TO 8 SERVINGS

This traditional appetizer is served at all Jewish celebrations, especially the life-cycle events. Somewhere I remember reading, "A taste of chopped liver brings a memory": a cousin's bar or bat mitzvah, Uncle Sam's wedding, your nephew's *bris,* or Sabbath meals shared with family and friends. Chicken fat, or *schmaltz* (SHMOLL-ts), as it's called in Yiddish, can be purchased at a kosher butcher shop, but it's not difficult to make your own (see page 139).

1 pound chicken livers

2 tablespoons vegetable oil

1 tablespoon chicken fat (schmaltz)

1 large onion, thinly sliced

4 large eggs, hard-cooked and quartered

1/4 cup mayonnaise

Salt and freshly ground black pepper
   to taste

Lettuce leaves (optional)

Olive slice or bit of fresh parsley for
   garnish

1. Preheat the broiler. Rinse the chicken livers in cold water and drain on paper towels. Remove the membranes and fat from the chicken livers and place the livers on a broiler pan. Broil 5 to 6 inches from the heat for 3 to 5 minutes per side or until no trace of redness remains. Set aside to cool.

2. In a medium skillet over medium heat, combine the vegetable oil and chicken fat. Add the onion and cook until lightly browned, 5 to 6 minutes.

3. Place the livers and eggs in the bowl of a food processor (see Note) and pulse until chopped medium coarse. Scrape the onions and fat from the skillet into the processor bowl and pulse several times, scraping the bowl as necessary.

4. Add the mayonnaise, salt, and pepper. Process just until mixed. Remove to a medium bowl. Taste to correct the seasonings, then cover and refrigerate. Serve on lettuce cups, if desired, and garnish with a slice of olive or a bit of parsley.

Note: *A meat or food grinder can be used to chop and blend everything together. Fold in the mayonnaise after the livers, eggs, and onion are ground together. A blender doesn't work with this recipe.*

EASY CHOPPED HERRING

MAKES 6 TO 8 SERVINGS

This mixture has better flavor and consistency when prepared with a food processor. You can also use a meat grinder. The chopped herring can be made a day or two ahead and refrigerated.

One 8-ounce jar pickled herring in
   wine sauce
1 cup crushed matzos
1 medium, tart apple, peeled and diced
1 medium onion, peeled and diced
1 teaspoon sugar
Salt and freshly ground black pepper
   to taste
3 large eggs, hard-cooked and quartered

1. Drain the liquid from the herring into a small bowl. Add the crushed matzos to the liquid.

2. Place the herring, matzo mixture, apple, and onion in the bowl of a food processor. Pulse 3 or 4 times, scraping the bowl as needed. Add the sugar, salt, and pepper. Pulse 2 times or until the herring mixture is chopped to a medium consistency. Remove to a medium glass bowl.

3. Place the eggs in the work bowl of the food processor. Pulse several times. Process until the eggs are the consistency of fine bread crumbs. Remove from the processor bowl and fold into the herring mixture. Transfer to a serving dish or an oiled 1-quart mold. Refrigerate for several hours or overnight.

ENDIVE NIBBLERS

MAKES APPROXIMATELY 12 LARGE LEAVES

Talk about a quick and easy appetizer. You can't beat this one. Fill the endive leaves with kosher whitefish spread or any of your favorite homemade fish pâtés or cheese spreads.

1 large head Belgian endive
One 7-ounce jar whitefish spread
Watercress for garnish

Pull individual leaves from the head of endive. Spread a small amount of whitefish spread in the center of each leaf and place on a platter garnished with watercress.

OLIVE SPREAD

MAKES 1 CUP

This is one of my favorite appetizers. I serve it with mini matzo crackers or use the spread as a filling in cherry tomatoes. It is both colorful and tasty.

One 19-ounce can Israeli cracked green olives
1 teaspoon dried oregano
1/2 teaspoon dried basil
1 tablespoon olive oil
1 tablespoon drained capers
1 tablespoon dry white wine

Drain and pit the olives. Place the olives and remaining ingredients in the food processor or blender. Process or blend until the mixture is the consistency of heavy caviar. Transfer to a small bowl; cover and refrigerate.

Passover Pizza

Makes 12 servings

This makes a great snack, hors d'oeuvre, or lunch entrée. Your children or grandchildren will love this pizza. Don't tell them what's in it; they'll never know they're eating vegetables. I like using Roma tomatoes when they're in season. Cut the pizza into smaller pieces for an hors d'oeuvre.

3 to 4 medium zucchini, grated (3 cups)

3 large eggs, beaten

1 cup matzo cake meal

1/2 teaspoon salt

2 cups grated mozzarella cheese

1 cup sliced black or green olives

2/3 cup finely chopped green onions

1/2 cup finely chopped red bell pepper

1 teaspoon dried oregano

1 teaspoon chopped fresh basil

3 medium, ripe tomatoes, thinly sliced

1. Preheat the oven to 450°F. Grease a 9×13-inch glass casserole. Place the grated zucchini in a strainer and press hard to remove the excess liquid, or wrap the zucchini in a dish towel and twist the towel, extracting the excess liquid.

2. In a medium bowl, combine the zucchini with the eggs, matzo cake meal, and salt. Mix well and spread evenly in the bottom of the casserole. Bake this crust for 8 minutes. Remove from the oven and allow it to cool for about 10 minutes. Lower the oven temperature to 350°F.

3. Layer the remaining ingredients over the entire zucchini crust in the following order: cheese, olives, green onions, and red bell pepper. Sprinkle with the oregano and basil. Arrange the tomato slices in even rows. Sprinkle lightly with salt, if desired. Bake for 20 minutes or until the cheese is bubbling. Remove from the oven and let cool for at least 5 minutes before slicing. Serve at once.

SALMON PÂTÉ

MAKES 4 TO 6 SERVINGS

This is an excellent substitute for gefilte fish or chopped liver. It's a terrific nosh and makes a great party hors d'oeuvre as a spread on mini matzo crackers.

1 small onion, peeled

1/4 cup (firmly packed) stemmed fresh parsley

8 ounces fresh salmon fillet, poached

4 ounces (1 stick) margarine, cut into 6 pieces

2 teaspoons freshly squeezed lemon juice

Pinch of cayenne pepper

Freshly ground black pepper to taste

1 teaspoon salt

1/2 cup toasted pecans (see Brown Sugar Meringue Crisps, page 91, to toast pecans)

1. Cut the onion in half. With the food processor motor running, drop the onion and parsley through the feed tube. Process until finely chopped.

2. Flake the salmon and add it to the processor bowl. Process for 15 seconds. Scrape the bowl. Add the margarine, lemon juice, cayenne pepper, black pepper, and salt. Pulse several times, then process for 10 seconds.

3. Scrape the bowl and add the pecans. Process 15 seconds longer. Remove the salmon from the bowl; place in a lightly oiled small gelatin mold or bowl; cover and refrigerate.

4. Chill the pâté for several hours or overnight. Serve on a lettuce-lined plate with miniature matzos, or use it to fill mini matzo puffs (see page 85).

Note: To poach a salmon, place 2 cups of water (or 1 cup water and 1 cup dry white wine), plus 1 teaspoon of whole pickling spices (or fresh dill) and the juice of 1 lemon in a covered skillet. Bring to a boil, reduce heat to a simmer, and add the salmon. Cover skillet and simmer (do not boil) for 8 to 10 minutes, until flesh turns from translucent to opaque and flakes easily when tested with a fork at the thickest part.

SEPHARDIC SPICED NUTS

MAKES ABOUT 4 CUPS

A mixture of Sephardic spices turns a familiar wine accompaniment into an exotic taste experience. Use one kind of nuts or mix several kinds together. They taste better made a day ahead. Any nuts not used in the recipe should be frozen so they won't turn rancid.

1¹/2 pounds shelled nuts
2 tablespoons sunflower oil
1¹/4 tablespoons Sephardic Spice Mix
Kosher salt to taste

1. Preheat the oven to 325°F. Spread the nuts out in a single layer in a large, shallow pan with sides.

2. Mix the oil and spice mix together and pour over the nuts. Stir well with a wooden spoon. Bake for 15 to 20 minutes, stirring frequently. Check the nuts so they don't get too dark and burn.

3. Remove the pan from the oven and spread the nuts on paper towels. Sprinkle lightly with salt to taste. Store in a glass container.

SEPHARDIC SPICE MIX

1 teaspoon ground cinnamon
1/4 teaspoon ground cloves
1/4 teaspoon ground nutmeg
1/4 teaspoon ground cardamom
1/4 teaspoon ground ginger
1/4 teaspoon crushed dried bay leaves
1/4 teaspoon cracked black pepper

Mix all the ingredients together in a small jar and store covered in the refrigerator.

SYLVIA RAUCHMAN'S SWEET-AND-SOUR MEATBALLS

MAKES 50 TO 60 SMALL HORS D'OEUVRES

My friend Sylvia loves entertaining. She developed this Passover recipe years ago. The Passover pickled vegetables can be found on the shelf in your supermarket or deli. These give this Passover hors d'oeuvre its perfect flavor. I like to use a variety of ground meats, but you may wish to use only one type. This recipe can be doubled for a large crowd and freezes well.

SAUCE

1 cup pickled vegetables with liquid

3/4 cup firmly packed brown sugar

1 cup applesauce

1 cup cold water

8-ounce can tomato sauce

MEATBALLS

2 pounds ground meat (turkey, veal, beef, or a mix)

2 large eggs

1 small onion, minced

1/4 cup matzo meal

1/4 teaspoon cayenne pepper

1. Place the sauce ingredients in a large saucepan or a Dutch oven. Bring to a boil over medium-high heat. Reduce the heat to low and cook the sauce for 20 minutes.

2. Meanwhile, in a large bowl, mix the ground meat, eggs, onion, matzo meal, and cayenne pepper together. Form into small balls.

3. Add the meatballs to the pan with the sauce. Cover and cook over medium-low heat for 30 minutes. Gently shake the pan after 15 minutes so the meatballs on the top settle down into the sauce.

BLENDER BEET BORSCHT

MAKES 8 SERVINGS

Perfect for lunch or served in a punch bowl as a starter for a party.

One 32-ounce jar borscht with beets
1 cup sour cream, plus extra
    for garnish
1 medium cucumber, peeled, seeded,
    and cut into 2-inch pieces
2 green onions, sliced
Salt and freshly ground black
    pepper to taste

1. Pour half the liquid from the jar of borscht into a blender with 1/2 cup of the sour cream. Blend on low speed for 10 seconds.

2. Add the cucumber pieces and sliced green onion. Pulse 2 times, then blend on high speed for 5 seconds. Empty into a large glass container or pitcher. (The beets will stain a plastic container.)

3. Pour the remaining liquid from the jar and the beets into the blender with the remaining 1/2 cup sour cream. Blend on low speed for 10 seconds, then on high speed for 5 seconds. Empty into the large container. Season with salt and pepper to taste. Serve the borscht garnished with a dollop of sour cream.

COLD MELON AND YOGURT SOUP

MAKES 8 TO 10 SERVINGS

This refreshing fruit soup is a good alternative as a first course or appetizer. The pareve nondairy cream substitute works well should you be watching your calories.

2 cups cubed cantaloupe

1 cup orange juice

Juice and grated zest of 1 lemon

1/2 teaspoon ground cinnamon

1/2 cup heavy cream or pareve nondairy creamer

2 tablespoons honey

Pinch of ground cumin

Two 8-ounce cartons peach yogurt

Chopped fresh mint for garnish

1. Place the cantaloupe cubes in the bowl of a food processor or blender. Pulse several times. Add the orange juice, lemon juice and zest, and cinnamon. Process or blend until smooth, 10 to 15 seconds.

2. Add the cream or nondairy creamer, honey, and cumin. Process or blend until smooth, scraping down the sides of the work bowl as necessary. Empty into a medium bowl and fold in the yogurt.

3. Cover and refrigerate for several hours or overnight. Serve very cold, garnished with fresh mint. This can also be served in a punch bowl along with your appetizers.

CREAM OF TOMATO SOUP

MAKES 6 SERVINGS

In a matter of minutes, you'll have soup for lunch or dinner.

*Three 10³/4-ounce cans condensed
    tomato soup*

1 tablespoon dried oregano

1 tablespoon dried basil

Pinch of cayenne pepper

*One 15-ounce can diced tomatoes,
    drained*

*2 cups whole milk or pareve nondairy
    creamer*

*Salt and freshly ground black pepper
    to taste*

*Sour cream or chopped parsley for
    garnish*

1. Empty 1 can of soup into a blender (see Note). Add the oregano, basil, and cayenne pepper. Blend until well mixed. Empty into a large bowl.

2. Add the tomatoes to the blender with the second can of tomato soup. Pulse several times. Add to the bowl.

3. Empty the third can of tomato soup into the blender. Add the milk or nondairy creamer and salt and pepper. Pulse several times or until well blended. Add to the soup in the bowl. Mix everything well. Taste to correct the seasonings.

4. In a microwave-safe 3-quart bowl, microwave the soup on high for 2 minutes. Stir and cook 3 more minutes. Garnish with a dollop of sour cream or freshly chopped parsley.

*Note: If you don't have a blender, use an electric
    mixer or handheld mixer. Blend everything
    together. Pour into a large saucepan over
    medium-high heat and heat just until the
    soup comes to a boil. Serve immediately.*

CUCUMBER-MINT SOUP

MAKES 6 SERVINGS

Fresh mint gives this soup the taste of spring.

*Two 10-ounce cans condensed cream of
   potato soup*

2 tablespoons chopped fresh mint

One 3-ounce package cream cheese

1/4 cup chopped fresh chives

*1 English cucumber, chopped but not
   peeled*

1/2 cup light sour cream

Pinch of cayenne pepper

1/8 teaspoon ground cumin

*Salt and freshly ground black pepper
   to taste*

*Finely chopped fresh mint for
   garnish*

1. Place 1 can of the potato soup and the mint, cream cheese, and chives in a blender or food processor. Blend until smooth. Empty into a large container.

2. Place the remaining can of potato soup and the cucumber, sour cream, cayenne pepper, cumin, salt, and pepper in the blender. Pulse several times, then process or blend until smooth. Add to the soup in the container. Cover and refrigerate for several hours or overnight. Serve in mugs. Garnish with chopped mint.

ROASTED SWEET BELL PEPPER SOUP

MAKES EIGHT 1-CUP SERVINGS

I was planning to serve soup as the entrée for a benefit party I held in my home. The produce store had a bin filled with red, orange, and yellow bell peppers. They were on sale at a great price, and I couldn't resist the challenge to create something new. This may seem a "busy" soup, but Passover is a busy time and it's worth every minute.

2 large heads of garlic

2 tablespoons olive oil

2 large red bell peppers

1 large yellow bell pepper

1 large orange bell pepper

2 small onions, chopped

2 tablespoons chopped fresh parsley

1 teaspoon each chopped fresh thyme,
    fennel, and summer savory, or
    1/2 teaspoon dried

4 cups boiling water

2 tablespoons pareve instant chicken-soup mix

1/4 teaspoon steak sauce

1/4 teaspoon paprika

Salt and freshly ground black pepper
    to taste

1/8 teaspoon cayenne pepper

2 medium new potatoes, peeled

Roasting the Garlic

1. Preheat the oven to 425°F. Prepare the garlic by removing only the loose, papery skins. Cut 1/2 inch from the top of the garlic heads to expose the cloves and discard it.

2. Rub the garlic heads with a little olive oil and set them in the center of a large piece of aluminum foil. Drizzle a little more olive oil over the top, then enclose the heads completely in the foil.

3. Place the foil packets on a cookie sheet in the middle of the oven and roast for 20 to 25 minutes. Unwrap the garlic, brush with olive oil, and continue roasting, uncovered, 10 to 15 more minutes. Allow the heads to cool for about 10 minutes before carefully squeezing out the roasted garlic cloves into a small container. Cover and refrigerate until ready to use. This can be done 1 or 2 days ahead.

Roasting the Bell Peppers

1. Preheat the broiler. Rub the peppers with a little olive oil. Place them on foil under the broiler. Broil about 6 inches from the heat source, turning often, until skins are charred on all sides.

2. Remove the peppers from the broiler and place them in a brown bag. Seal the bag and allow the peppers to steam for 10 to 15 minutes.

3. Remove the peppers from the bag; peel the charred black skins from the peppers. Using a paring knife, remove the stem ends and the seeds. You can place the peppers in a bowl and cover with a little olive oil until you are ready to use them. The peppers can be roasted several days ahead and refrigerated. Be sure to drain the peppers and pat them dry with paper towels before using.

Preparing the Soup

1. Heat the oil in a large nonstick stockpot over medium heat, add the onions and parsley, and sauté until the onions begin to wilt. Add the thyme, fennel, and summer savory and sauté 2 to 3 minutes more.

2. Puree the garlic and roasted bell peppers together in a food processor or blender and add the puree to the onion mixture. Sauté for 2 to 3 minutes.

3. In a 4-cup measure, mix the instant soup mix with 2 cups of the boiling water. Add to the roasted vegetable mixture along with the remaining ingredients. Bring to a boil over high heat. Reduce heat to low and simmer for 25 to 30 minutes or until the potatoes are soft.

4. In a large bowl, strain the liquid from the vegetables and return liquid to stockpot. Puree the vegetables in a food processor or blender and return to the pot, stirring until well combined. Mix in the remaining 2 cups of boiling water. Taste and add more salt, pepper, or cayenne as needed.

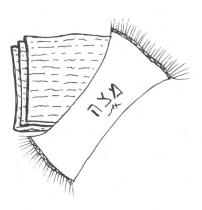

EGG DROP SOUP

MAKES 4 TO 6 SERVINGS

You may wish to add a little cubed cooked chicken or freshly chopped parsley for extra flavor and color. The eggs are added just before serving.

8 cups chicken broth, homemade
*   or canned*
Salt and ground white pepper
*   to taste*
3 large eggs, at room temperature

1. Heat the chicken broth in a large nonreactive saucepan or pot over medium-high heat until it begins to boil. Turn the heat to medium-low and season with salt and white pepper. Simmer for 10 to 15 minutes. Remove from the heat.

2. In a small bowl, whisk the eggs to blend. Slowly whisk about 1 cup of the hot soup into the eggs.

3. Stirring constantly, gradually pour the egg mixture into the soup. Return the pot to the stove and cook over low heat, whisking constantly, until the soup is thickened slightly, about 1 minute. Remove from the heat. Do not allow the soup to cook after the eggs have been added, or they will curdle. Serve at once.

SHERRIED MUSHROOM SOUP

MAKES 8 TO 10 SERVINGS

A few additions by the cook transforms packaged mushroom soup mix into a sophisticated dinner course.

Four 2¹/₈-ounce packages instant mushroom soup mix

3 cups boiling water

1 pound fresh mushrooms

3 tablespoons margarine or butter

2 teaspoons freshly squeezed lemon juice

2 cups heavy cream or milk

¹/₄ cup sherry

Pinch of ground white pepper

1. Pour the soup mix into a large container. Add the water and stir well. Set aside.

2. Wipe the mushrooms with a damp paper towel, then slice them. Melt the margarine in a large stockpot, add the mushrooms, and cook over medium heat for 2 minutes, shaking the pan. As the mushrooms begin to soften, add the lemon juice. Increase heat to high and cook, stirring constantly, for about 2 minutes. Remove the mushrooms with a slotted spoon and set them aside.

3. Reduce the heat to medium, pour the soup mix liquid into the stockpot, and let it come to a slow boil, stirring constantly. Remove the pan from the heat and add the cream or milk, reserved mushrooms, sherry, and white pepper. Stir well. Place the pan back on low heat for 3 to 4 minutes, stirring constantly. Do not let the soup boil. Serve at once.

VEGETARIAN BORSCHT

MAKES 5 QUARTS

This is a good make-ahead soup that can be made quickly in the food processor. It gets thicker the longer it sits. This also freezes well. Those of Ashkenazic background can leave out the green beans.

2 medium onions, peeled

3 ribs celery, with tops

1 leek, white part only

6 to 8 carrots, peeled

1/4 cup margarine

3 large potatoes, peeled

2 medium turnips, peeled

3 medium parsnips, peeled

1 pound green beans

1 bunch watercress, stems removed

1 small head cabbage, cored and cut into 4 wedges

2 tablespoons tomato paste

4 teaspoons salt

1/4 teaspoon ground white pepper

1. Place the slicing disk into the bowl of the food processor. Cut the onions, celery, leek, and carrots to fit feed tube. With light pressure, push the vegetables through the feed tube using the pusher.

2. Over medium heat, melt the margarine in a large stockpot. Add the onions, celery, leeks, and carrots and sauté until the onion is soft and limp, 3 to 5 minutes. Remove the pot from the heat.

3. Insert the French-fry blade into the food processor. Cut the potatoes, turnips, and parsnips to fit the feed tube. Chop, using the pusher with firm pressure. Add these vegetables to the stockpot.

4. Insert the metal blade into the food processor bowl. Add the green beans and watercress. Pulse several times to chop, then add to the stockpot.

5. Place 2 wedges of the cabbage into the processor bowl. Chop with several pulses. Add to the stockpot. Repeat with the remaining cabbage and add to the stockpot. Add the tomato paste, salt, and white pepper to the stockpot.

6. Add enough cold water to cover the vegetables, and bring to a boil over high heat. Reduce heat to low and simmer, covered, for 1 hour. Serve hot.

ZUCCHINI BISQUE

MAKES ABOUT 2 QUARTS

This recipe came to me from Sue Teller, an outstanding Cincinnati cook and community volunteer. We share creative fund-raising and food ideas.

1/2 cup (1 stick) margarine or butter

1 medium onion, chopped

6 cups grated unpeeled zucchini (about 11/2 pounds)

21/2 cups chicken broth made from pareve instant chicken soup mix

2 teaspoons dried basil

1/2 teaspoon ground nutmeg

1 teaspoon salt

Freshly ground black pepper to taste

1 cup milk or cream

1. In a large stockpot, melt the margarine over medium heat. Add the onion and sauté until limp. Add the grated zucchini and pareve chicken broth. Reduce heat to low and simmer, covered, for 15 minutes.

2. Transfer the mixture to a food processor or blender in 2 batches; puree. Add the basil, nutmeg, salt, and pepper. Pulse several times.

3. Pour mixture into a large bowl. Add the milk or cream and stir until well blended. Serve hot or cold.

Note: If you freeze this for later use, give it a good whirl in your processor or blender after thawing.

ARTICHOKE ANTIPASTO SALAD

MAKES 8 SERVINGS

This salad is very filling and has all the goodies you'd find on any Italian antipasto platter. If serving dairy, include the cheese and eliminate the summer sausage. If serving meat, use the sausage and eliminate the cheese. Serve this at room temperature or chilled.

One 14-ounce can artichoke hearts

1 roasted red bell pepper, cut into strips (see Sephardic Salade Shackshooka, page 46, to roast peppers)

4 ounces provolone cheese, cut into thin strips

4 ounces beef summer sausage, sliced and halved

3 ounces pitted black olives, sliced

1/4 cup olive oil

1 tablespoon balsamic vinegar

1 tablespoon red wine vinegar

1/4 teaspoon dried basil, or 1/4 cup thinly sliced fresh

1/4 teaspoon dried oregano, or 1/4 cup chopped fresh

Salt and freshly ground black pepper to taste

Chopped fresh parsley for garnish

1. Drain the artichoke hearts, rinse in cold water, pat dry with paper towels, and slice into a large bowl. Add the roasted red pepper, cheese, sausage, and olives.

2. In a small bowl, combine the olive oil, vinegars, basil, oregano, salt, and pepper. Mix until well blended. Add to the artichoke mixture. Toss and sprinkle with parsley.

CARROT-RAISIN SALAD

MAKES 8 SERVINGS

I adapted Jane Armstrong's recipe from *Salads—Food Writers' Favorites,* a cookbook benefiting Mother's Against Drunk Driving. My family prefers mayonnaise and raisins rather than the vegetable oil and currants called for in the original recipe. This is a great favorite with my grandchildren.

1/4 *cup dark raisins*

2 cups coarsely shredded carrots

2 tablespoons freshly squeezed lemon juice

1 teaspoon grated lemon zest

1/4 *cup freshly squeezed orange juice*

1/2 *cup mayonnaise*

1/2 *teaspoon sugar*

Freshly ground black pepper to taste

1. In a small bowl filled with hot water, soften the raisins for 5 minutes.

2. In a large bowl, combine the carrots, lemon juice, lemon zest, and orange juice. Mix well. Drain the raisins. Fold them into the carrots along with the mayonnaise, sugar, and pepper. Mix well. Refrigerate, covered, several hours before serving.

FOUR BELL PEPPER SALAD

MAKES 6 SERVINGS

I try to keep several roasted bell peppers in my freezer. I use the frozen peppers whenever I need them for soup, salad dressings, or casseroles. Peppers can be roasted and kept in the refrigerator for approximately 1 week. Pour a small amount of olive oil on top of the roasted pepper, and refrigerate, covered.

1 clove garlic, minced

3 tablespoons freshly squeezed lemon juice

1/2 cup olive oil

*Salt and freshly ground black pepper
    to taste*

*4 medium bell peppers, preferably red,
    yellow, orange, and green, roasted (see
    Sephardic Salade Shackshooka, page 46,
    to roast peppers)*

1 green onion

Black olives and capers for garnish

1. In a food processor or blender, add the garlic, lemon juice, olive oil, salt, and pepper. Process or blend for 3 to 5 seconds. Set aside.

2. Cut peppers into strips about 1/4 inch wide and place in a serving dish. Cut the green onion into thin diagonal slices and sprinkle over the peppers. Pour the dressing over the peppers. Marinate at room temperature until serving time. Garnish with black olives and capers.

GINGER CHICKEN SALAD

MAKES 6 SERVINGS

The ginger in this main-course salad adds a satisfying taste to this quickly prepared recipe.

2 tablespoons vegetable oil

1 teaspoon grated fresh ginger, or 1/2 teaspoon ground ginger

1 clove garlic, minced

1 pound boneless, skinless chicken breasts, cut into 1-inch cubes

Salt and freshly ground black pepper to taste

1 tablespoon freshly squeezed lemon juice

1/2 cup regular or light mayonnaise

1 mango, peeled and diced

1/2 cup diced celery

1/4 cup chopped fresh chives

1/2 cup minced fresh parsley for garnish

1. Heat the oil in a large skillet over medium-high heat. Add the ginger, garlic, chicken, salt, and pepper; sauté until the chicken is cooked through, 3 to 4 minutes. Remove the chicken to a salad bowl.

2. Add the lemon juice to the skillet. Over high heat, scrape up the brown bits from the bottom of the skillet. Pour into a 1-cup measure.

3. Combine the mayonnaise with the lemon juice mixture. Add to the chicken and toss. Add the mango, celery, and chives; mix well. Cover and refrigerate for several hours before serving. Garnish with parsley.

HERBED POTATO SALAD

MAKES 6 SERVINGS

Spring and Passover bring a large variety of fresh herbs. I look forward to preparing this salad as a vegetarian entrée. It's quite filling. If desired, you can add a hard-boiled egg to the salad mixture.

2 pounds red-skinned potatoes,
    cooked and sliced but not peeled

3 ribs celery, thinly sliced (about 1 cup)

1/4 cup broken pecans

3/4 cup mayonnaise

1/2 cup sour cream or nonfat yogurt

2 tablespoons chopped fresh chives

1/2 teaspoon chopped fresh
    winter savory

2 teaspoons chopped fresh basil,
    or 1 teaspoon dried

Grated zest of 1 lemon

1 tablespoon balsamic vinegar

2 tablespoons prepared horseradish

Salt and freshly ground black
    pepper to taste

1 bunch watercress, chopped,
    for garnish

1. Place the sliced potatoes in a large bowl. Add the celery and pecans.

2. In a separate small bowl, mix the mayonnaise and sour cream with the chives, savory, basil, lemon zest, vinegar, and horseradish until blended. Add the salt and pepper.

3. Fold the mayonnaise mixture into the potatoes. Refrigerate, covered, for 2 hours or longer. To serve, distribute the watercress over the bottom of a serving platter. Gently mix the potato salad and mound on top.

TUNA SALAD FOR KIDS

MAKES 1 1/2 CUPS

Healthy, quick, and kids love it. A gift from David Warda, a talented Cincinnati chef, cookbook author, and costume designer.

One 6-ounce can water-packed tuna

3/4 cup finely grated carrots

1/2 teaspoon sweet relish

1/4 teaspoon prepared horseradish

Pinch of dried dill

1 heaping tablespoon mayonnaise, or as needed

Drain the tuna and place in a small bowl. Add the grated carrots, relish, horseradish, and dill. Fold in the mayonnaise. Be sure to use enough mayonnaise to moisten and hold the tuna together. Refrigerate, covered, at least 1 hour.

WARM TURKEY SALAD

MAKES 6 SERVINGS

The new craze of mixing warm turkey or seafood with cold greens is a great way to use up leftover turkey breast. I served this salad as an entrée for a ladies' luncheon.

4 to 5 cups chopped cooked turkey breast
    (bite-size pieces)

1/2 cup pecan halves

1 cup sliced fresh mushrooms

1 to 1 1/2 cups red wine vinaigrette dressing
    (see Note)

1 bunch fresh watercress, chopped

1 small head romaine lettuce, torn into
    bite-size pieces

2 cups sliced celery cabbage or bok choy

1 small head radicchio

1 small head Belgian endive

1. In a medium bowl, mix the turkey, pecan halves, mushrooms, and vinaigrette dressing. Let marinate in the refrigerator for 1 to 2 hours.

2. Place the watercress, romaine lettuce, and celery cabbage in the bottom of a large salad bowl. Separate the leaves of the radicchio and endive. Distribute them around the sides of the salad bowl.

3. Remove the marinated turkey mixture from the refrigerator and place in a large saucepan. Heat over medium heat for 8 to 10 minutes or until heated through, adding more vinaigrette dressing if needed. Remove the warm turkey mixture with a slotted spoon and set in the center of the salad greens. Pour the warmed dressing evenly over the top of the salad.

Note: Use the recipe for Balsamic Vinaigrette Dressing on page 31 to make the dressing. Substitute red wine vinegar for the balsamic.

EASY HOLLANDAISE

MAKES APPROXIMATELY 1 CUP

My laundress, Margaret Green, also a great cook, shared this recipe with me. I usually double the recipe when making it. This Hollandaise can be prepared ahead, covered, refrigerated, and reheated over low heat in a double boiler.

4 large egg yolks

1 teaspoon solid vegetable shortening

Juice of 2 lemons

1/2 cup (1 stick) butter or margarine, or use half of each

Combine all the ingredients in the top of a double boiler placed over simmering water. Turn the heat to medium-high. Stir sauce continuously with a wire whisk until it begins to thicken to desired consistency. Remove the pan from the heat.

FRUIT TARTAR SAUCE

MAKES APPROXIMATELY 1 CUP

This sauce is delicious over sautéed tuna steaks or grilled fish. It can also be used as a delightfully different dip with raw vegetables. The recipe can be easily be doubled.

1/4 cup regular or low-fat mayonnaise

1/4 cup regular or low-fat sour cream

1/4 cup chopped fresh mango (see Note)

1 teaspoon grated orange zest

3 tablespoons chopped red or Vidalia onion

1 tablespoon minced fresh mint

1 tablespoon freshly squeezed orange juice

Combine all the ingredients in a small bowl, mixing well. For the best flavor, cover and refrigerate for 30 minutes or more before serving. The sauce is best served on the same day it is prepared.

Note: If mangos are unavailable, diced orange sections can be substituted.

ORANGE SAUCE FOR SPONGE CAKE

MAKES APPROXIMATELY 2 CUPS

Each Passover, Pearl Simon's family looks forward to enjoying this orange sauce over their sponge cake. My family likes it over fresh sliced oranges and pineapple.

2 tablespoons potato starch
2 cups store-bought orange juice
1 cup sugar
2 large navel oranges,
*   thinly sliced*

1. Place the potato starch in a 1-cup measure. Add 1 tablespoon of the orange juice and mix well, dissolving the potato starch.

2. Place the remaining orange juice and the sugar in a medium saucepan. Whisk in the potato starch mixture. Heat over medium-high heat 5 to 6 minutes, or until thickened. Add the orange slices. Let cool slightly and serve over sponge cake.

Variation
You may wish to add a little Passover brandy or liqueur with the orange juice before heating the sauce.

Schmaltz

(Rendered Chicken Fat)

Makes approximately 1/2 cup

I prepare a small amount of *schmaltz* (SHMOLL-ts) each Passover. It keeps for several months in the refrigerator and freezes well. Since everyone is watching their fat intake, I never add more than about 1 tablespoon to the recipes. I feel it provides a little traditional *tam* (TOM), or flavor. It is preferable to use the fat and skin from a stewing or soup chicken.

1 cup uncooked pieces of solid chicken fat,
    cut into 1/2-inch pieces
Skin from 1 whole chicken breast, cut into
    1/4-inch pieces
1 tablespoon grated onion

1. Rinse the pieces of chicken fat and skin in cold water. Pat dry with paper towels. Place in a small skillet and cook over medium heat until they begin to sizzle and the skin begins to be barely brown, 5 to 10 minutes.

2. Add the onion and reduce the heat to low. Cook for about 10 minutes to render the chicken fat, turning some of the larger pieces of fat from time to time with a wooden spoon for even browning. The skin should become crisp and brown.

3. Pour through a strainer over a small bowl. Drain the skin, or *gribenes* (GRIB-ends), on paper towels. Let the rendered fat cool before placing it in a glass container. Cover and refrigerate for up to a week, or place in a freezer container and freeze.

Note: The gribenes *don't keep well. It's better to enjoy them immediately on a good piece of rye bread, assuming you're making this before Passover. Otherwise, eat them on miniature matzos.*

SALSA FOR KIDS

MAKES 1 CUP

David Warda loves working with kids. He's a Cincinnati author, theater major, and former New York chef. He shared this recipe with me when I was interviewing him for my column, "The Modern Jewish Cook," in *The American Israelite*. It's great for kids because they can help with the preparation and the flavors are not too spicy.

One 16-ounce can stewed tomatoes
One 10-ounce jar chunky salsa

Place the ingredients in a blender or food processor and pulse 2 or 3 times. This sauce needs to remain a little chunky, so don't overprocess it. Place in a covered container and refrigerate.

VANILLA SAUCE

MAKES APPROXIMATELY 3 CUPS

This sauce is wonderful over fruit or cake. It's a great way to use up egg yolks left over from recipes that call for whites only.

5 large egg yolks
3/4 cup sugar
Pinch of salt
3 cups milk, heated
1 teaspoon vanilla extract

1. In a 4-cup measure, beat the eggs slightly with a fork. Over medium-high heat, place in the top of a double boiler set over simmering water and stir in the sugar and salt.

2. Stirring constantly, slowly add the hot milk. Cook until the mixture begins to thicken. Add the vanilla, and continue stirring until the sauce leaves a good coating on a wooden spoon. Serve immediately or place in a bowl, cover with plastic wrap, and store in the refrigerator.

VERY BERRY SAUCE

MAKES 2 CUPS

A quick and easy topping for ice cream, sorbet, fruit, or pound cake. This can be doubled and freezes well.

1 pint fresh raspberries, or 12 ounces frozen unsweetened raspberries

1 pint fresh strawberries, sliced, or 10 ounces frozen unsweetened strawberries

1 cup sugar

2 tablespoons freshly squeezed orange juice

2 tablespoons orange-flavored liqueur (optional)

Press the raspberries through a fine sieve or food mill over a large bowl to remove the seeds. Working in batches, place the sieved raspberries, strawberries, and sugar in a food processor or blender. Pulse several times. Process or blend for 10 seconds. Add the orange juice and liqueur (if using). Process or blend 10 seconds more. Remove and refrigerate, covered, until ready to use.

BLINTZES, BLINTZES, AND MORE BLINTZES

MAKES 12 TO 14 BLINTZES

Jewish blintzes, Chinese eggrolls, or Spanish *pastilla*—whatever you wish to call them—they're pastry leaves or crêpes wrapped around a filling. This basic recipe for Passover crêpes can be used with a variety of fillings. Spinach or meat can be substituted for the traditional cheese filling (see page 144). I usually double the recipes and freeze the blintzes to use weeks later.

CRÊPES

3 large eggs

1/2 teaspoon salt

1 1/2 cups cold water

2/3 cup matzo cake meal

1/2 cup melted margarine or vegetable oil, or as needed

CHEESE FILLING

One 8-ounce package farmer cheese

One 8-ounce package cream cheese

One 12-ounce container cottage cheese

3 large egg yolks

2 tablespoons sugar

1/4 teaspoon ground cinnamon or dried lemon peel

1 teaspoon vanilla extract or freshly squeezed lemon juice

Making the Crêpes

1. In a medium bowl, combine the eggs, salt, and water. Gradually add the cake meal. Beat until smooth. This can be done in a food processor or blender or by hand in a medium bowl. Place in the refrigerator while preparing the filling.

2. Make any one of the fillings below and keep it in the refrigerator.

Cheese Filling: Processor Method

1. Cut the farmer cheese and cream cheese into small pieces. Place in a food processor, add the cottage cheese, and pulse several times. Process until smooth, scraping down the sides.

2. In a 2-cup measure, mix the egg yolks, sugar, cinnamon or lemon peel, and vanilla or lemon juice. With the processor running, pour the egg yolk mixture through the feed tube into the cheese mixture. Empty into a large bowl, cover, and refrigerate while cooking the leaves or crêpes.

Cheese Filling: Conventional Method

Use an electric mixer. In a mixer bowl, beat the cheeses first, then add the remaining ingredients and mix on medium speed until smooth.

Cooking the Crêpes

1. Remove the batter from the refrigerator. Place the melted margarine or vegetable oil in a cup alongside the crêpe pan. Use a small crêpe pan.

2. Brush the pan with a little melted margarine or vegetable oil and place over medium-high heat. Let the oil begin to bubble. Pour in enough batter to just cover the bottom of the pan. Swirl the pan around and cook the crêpe until the moisture is gone from the top or the crêpe begins to pull away from the sides of the pan, curling a little on the edges, 20 to 30 seconds on one side only.

3. Turn the crêpe onto a cutting board covered with waxed paper. The crêpes may be stacked one upon the other.

Filling, Frying, and Serving the Blintzes

1. Remove the filling from the refrigerator. Fill one blintz at a time. On the cooked side, near the edge of the crêpe, place a large tablespoon of filling. Turn the edge over the filling; fold in the sides so they overlap; roll to the end like a jelly roll. Continue using the crêpes and the filling in this manner until both are used up. The blintzes can be frozen at this point if you wish (see Note).

2. Place the blintzes seam side down in a large greased skillet. Fry over medium-high heat until blintzes are crisp and golden brown, approximately 2 to 3 minutes on each side. Or bake in a preheated 425°F oven in a single layer on a lightly greased cookie sheet, brushing the tops with melted margarine or a little oil. Bake the blintzes 15 to 20 minutes.

3. Serve the cheese blintzes with sour cream or fruit sauce and the spinach or meat blintzes with any leftover cooked Passover gravy.

Note: You can freeze the blintzes in a single row on a cookie sheet in 2 to 3 hours. Then place in a sealed plastic bag and leave in the freezer until needed.

continues

Variations

SPINACH FILLING

3 tablespoons margarine

1/2 pound mushrooms, chopped

1 medium onion, finely chopped

1 1/2 pounds fresh spinach, cooked, drained, and
    finely chopped

Salt and freshly ground black pepper to taste

1 teaspoon ground nutmeg

Processor Method

1. Melt the margarine in a small skillet over
    medium-high heat. Add the mushrooms and
    onion and sauté until the onion wilts, about
    5 minutes. Set aside. Place the cooked spinach in
    the bowl of a food processor. Pulse several times.

2. Add the sautéed vegetables, salt, pepper, and
    nutmeg to the processor. Pulse several times or
    until well mixed. Empty into a large bowl.
    Refrigerate while cooking crêpes.

Conventional Method

Melt the margarine in a small skillet over
medium-high heat. Add the mushrooms and
onion and sauté until the onion wilts, about
5 minutes. In a large bowl, mix the spinach with
the sautéed vegetables, salt, pepper, and nutmeg. The consistency may not be as smooth,
but it will still work.

MEAT FILLING

3 cups small pieces of cooked leftover meat
    or chicken

1 small cooked potato, quartered

1/2 cup matzo meal

1/2 teaspoon salt

1/4 teaspoon cracked black pepper

1 large egg

1/4 cup leftover gravy or chicken broth

1 medium onion, quartered

Processor Method

Place the meat or chicken in the bowl of a
food processor. Process for 6 to 8 seconds.
Add the potato and pulse 1 or 2 times. Add the
remaining ingredients and process 3 to 4 seconds more. Refrigerate while cooking the
crêpes.

Conventional Method

Use a meat grinder to grind the meat, potato,
and onion together over a large bowl. Add the
remaining ingredients and mix well by hand.

CABBAGE ROLLS IN SWEET-AND-SOUR SAUCE

MAKES 6 TO 8 SERVINGS

The popularity of stuffed cabbage rolls extends beyond any special Jewish holiday. This happens to be Eileen Chalfie's recipe. An outstanding cook and baker, she is a member of my cookbook focus group. The cabbage rolls make a great lunch, as well as an entrée for dinner. They freeze well and can be made weeks ahead.

2 medium heads green cabbage (1¹/2 to
  2 pounds each)

FILLING

2 pounds extra-lean ground beef
1 tablespoon tomato paste
¹/2 teaspoon salt
1 medium onion, chopped
¹/8 teaspoon freshly ground black pepper
¹/3 cup matzo meal
1 large egg

SAUCE

Two 16-ounce cans whole cranberry sauce
1 jar chili sauce
³/4 cup freshly squeezed lemon juice

1. Core the cabbage and place in a 2-quart microwave-safe dish. Add 2 tablespoons water and cover with vented plastic wrap; microwave on high or until the cabbage leaves are soft, 6 to 8 minutes. Remove and let cool while making filling.

2. In a medium bowl, mix the filling ingredients together until well blended. Wet your hands with water and roll the meat filling into golf-ball-size portions.

3. Preheat the oven to 350°F. To make the sauce, combine all the sauce ingredients in a large bowl. Mix until the sauce is well blended. Set aside.

4. Gently pull the cabbages apart leaf by leaf until they become too small to fill. Lay a meatball in the center of a leaf. Fold each side of the cabbage leaf toward the center over the meat filling, then roll from the core end forward. You may wish to hold the leaf closed with a toothpick.

6. Place the cabbage rolls in a 9×13-inch glass baking pan. Continue until all the leaves are filled. You may have more filling than leaves. Just add the extra meatballs to the casserole as is.

7. Chop the remaining cabbage leaves and sprinkle over the top of the casserole. Cover with the sauce. Cover the pan with aluminum foil and bake for 2 hours. Baste 2 or 3 times during the cooking. Remove the toothpicks and serve with rice or mashed potatoes.

GLAZED SALMON

MAKES 8 SERVINGS

This salmon recipe is ideal for calorie counters, especially if you use low-fat mayonnaise. Spray the grill well with cooking spray before placing the salmon steaks on it, or use a wire grilling basket that has been well sprayed. You can also bake this in a 400°F oven.

1/4 cup mayonnaise

1/2 cup chopped pitted Greek olives

Juice and grated zest of 2 lemons

3 teaspoons minced fresh dill,
    or 2 teaspoons dried

Eight 4-ounce salmon steaks

1/4 cup olive oil

Fresh dill for garnish

1. Blend the mayonnaise, olives, lemon juice and zest, and dill together in a small bowl. Brush this mixture evenly over both sides of the salmon steaks.

2. Cover the steaks and place them in the refrigerator to marinate 30 minutes to an hour before grilling. Brush the grill with olive oil and preheat the grill to high heat. Cook the salmon until the fish flakes easily when tested with a fork, 2 to 4 minutes per side.

3. You can also bake the salmon steaks in a large, greased baking dish for 6 minutes on each side at 400°F. Transfer the steaks to a platter and garnish with sprigs of fresh dill.

HALIBUT STEAKS IN FOIL

MAKES 8 SERVINGS

Tired of meat and poultry? Try this flavorful fish recipe for a change of pace. It's steamed, baked, and served in its own foil pocket.

8 halibut steaks (about 1/3 pound each)

2/3 cup vegetable oil

Freshly ground black pepper to taste

2/3 cup dry white wine

1 teaspoon dried thyme, or 2 teaspoons fresh

1 teaspoon chopped fresh parsley

1 teaspoon dried rosemary, or 2 teaspoons fresh

1. Preheat the oven to 425°F. Wipe each halibut steak with paper towels. Place each steak on a piece of aluminum foil that has been cut into a rectangle large enough to hold it. Brush each steak with oil, then grind a little pepper over it.

2. In a 2-cup glass measure, mix the wine, thyme, parsley, and rosemary together. Brush evenly over each halibut steak. Fold up the foil and crimp the edges together tightly, sealing in the fish and making a pocket.

3. Place the foil packets on a cookie sheet and bake in the oven for 15 to 20 minutes or until the fish flakes when tested with a fork. Serve in the foil (see Note).

Note: You can prepare the fish in the foil earlier in the day, place in the refrigerator, then bake later. If using frozen halibut steaks, do not thaw them. Bake them 5 to 10 minutes longer.

LAKE TROUT BAKED IN WHITE WINE

MAKES 4 SERVINGS

If you're on a low-cholesterol diet, this just fits the bill for Passover. Be sure to ask your fishmonger to fillet the trout for you.

1/4 cup freshly squeezed lemon juice

3 pounds lake trout, boned and filleted

1 tablespoon chopped shallots

1 teaspoon dried thyme

Pinch of kosher salt

Pinch of ground white pepper

1/4 cup vegetable oil

1/2 cup white wine

1/4 cup skim milk

2 teaspoons margarine

1/2 teaspoon potato starch

*1 tablespoon grated
   Parmesan cheese (optional)*

1. Preheat the oven to 325°F. In a shallow pan, combine the lemon juice with a little cold water. Dip the trout in this mixture, coating both sides. Dry the trout well with paper towels and place in a 9 × 12-inch baking dish, skin side down.

2. Sprinkle the chopped shallots, thyme, salt, and pepper over the top surface of the fish. Add the oil and wine. Cover the trout with foil and bake for 15 to 20 minutes or until the fish flakes when tested with a fork and feels firm to the touch. Remove from the oven.

3. Empty the liquid from the baking pan into a 2-cup glass measure. Add the milk and set aside. Melt the margarine in a medium saucepan. Add the potato starch and stir well with a wire whisk. When it begins to bubble, add the milk mixture along with the cheese. Continue stirring until the sauce thickens. Pour over the fish and serve. For a little more color, place the fish under the broiler for a minute or two to top brown.

MARILYN'S LEAN LEMON-GLAZED MEAT LOAF

MAKES 6 SERVINGS

Over the years my friend Marilyn Harris and I have shared recipes and culinary stories whenever she has invited me to be a guest on her radio program, "Cooking with Marilyn." This is her recipe, which I adapted for Passover. It's a light, make-ahead entrée, and I always double the recipe and freeze a loaf. Be sure the ground beef and veal are the leanest you can find and use only ground turkey breast.

3 tablespoons olive oil

1 1/2 cups chopped onions

8 ounces very lean ground beef

1 pound ground turkey breast

8 ounces ground veal

1 large egg

2 large egg whites

2 tablespoons pareve milk substitute

1 cup ground soup nuts (mandlen)

1 large clove garlic, finely minced

1/4 cup chopped fresh rosemary

1/4 cup chopped fresh parsley

1 teaspoon salt, or to taste

1/4 teaspoon freshly ground black pepper

1 1/2 teaspoons finely chopped lemon zest

GLAZE

1/2 cup ketchup

2 tablespoons freshly squeezed lemon juice

2 tablespoons brown sugar

1/8 teaspoon cayenne pepper

1/4 teaspoon balsamic vinegar

1. Preheat the oven to 350°F. Heat the oil in a small skillet over medium-high heat. Add the chopped onions and sauté for about 3 minutes, stirring; remove from the heat and let cool.

2. In a large bowl, mix the ground beef, turkey, and veal together. With a fork, gently work the onions into the meat mixture.

3. In a 2-cup glass measure, whisk together the egg, egg whites, and pareve milk substitute. Pour over the ground soup nuts, mix well, and work into the meat mixture along with the garlic, rosemary, parsley, salt, pepper, and lemon zest.

4. Gently shape the meat mixture by pressing it into a nonstick (or lightly oiled) 9×5-inch loaf pan. Turn out onto a shallow baking pan.

5. In a small bowl, mix the glaze ingredients together with a whisk or fork. Spread evenly over the top and sides of the meat loaf.

6. Bake for 1 hour 15 minutes or until cooked through. Cool 5 to 10 minutes before slicing.

HACHIS PARMENTIER

(MOROCCAN SHEPHERD'S PIE)

MAKES 4 SERVINGS

Several years ago, while traveling throughout Morocco, we had this delicious entrée made with canned tuna at a restaurant in Casablanca. It reminded me of the shepherd's pie my mother used to make with leftover mashed potatoes. This is an excellent luncheon entrée for Passover. The recipe can be easily doubled.

4 Yukon gold or baking potatoes, boiled

1 large egg yolk

1/4 cup milk

Salt and freshly ground black pepper to taste

One 6-ounce can water-packed tuna

1 small onion, finely grated

1 teaspoon freshly squeezed lemon juice

1 teaspoon grated lemon zest

1/4 cup chopped fresh parsley

1/2 cup grated cheddar cheese (optional)

1. In a large bowl, mash the potatoes with the egg yolk, milk, salt, and pepper. Set aside.

2. Drain the tuna and flake it into a small bowl. Add the grated onion, lemon juice and zest, and parsley. Mix well. Set aside.

3. Preheat the oven to 350°F. Lightly grease an 8-inch square pan or 4 individual ramekins with vegetable oil.

4. Place half of the mashed potatoes on the bottom of the pan or ramekins.

5. Distribute the tuna mixture evenly over the potato layer. Spread the remaining mashed potatoes on top of the tuna and sprinkle with cheese, if desired. Bake for 30 minutes or until golden brown on top. Cut into squares and serve immediately.

Note: Use the back of the tines of a fork to smooth the layers of the mashed potatoes.

ORA'S BRISKET

MAKES 6 SERVINGS

This is an alternative way of roasting a brisket. If you have any left over, it makes outstanding barbecue sandwiches. Long, slow cooking adds to the flavor of the roast. This is a great make-ahead entrée.

3 pounds first-cut brisket

1 cup chili sauce

1/2 cup brown sugar

1/4 cup dry red wine

1/4 cup water

1 small or medium onion, sliced

3 whole cloves

6 whole black peppercorns

3 bay leaves

1. Preheat the oven to 325°F. Rinse the brisket and pat dry with paper towels. In a small bowl, combine the chili sauce, brown sugar, wine, and water. Mix well. Pour 1/4 of the chili sauce mixture into a roasting pan. Place the brisket on the sauce, fat side up. Distribute the onion, cloves, peppercorns, and bay leaves over brisket and top with the remaining chili sauce mixture. Cover tightly and bake for 50 to 55 minutes per pound or until the meat is fork-tender.

2. Remove the brisket from the pan and place in a container. Remove the bay leaves and any visible cloves or peppercorns from the natural gravy in the pan and place the gravy in an appropriate container. (If desired, the natural gravy and onions can be pureed in a food processor or blender.) Cover and refrigerate the brisket and the gravy for several hours or overnight.

3. To reheat the brisket for serving, slice it against the grain to the desired thickness and place in a casserole sprayed with nonstick spray. Remove and discard any congealed fat from the gravy mixture and pour the gravy over the brisket, discarding any cloves and peppercorns you find. Reheat, covered, in a 375°F oven for 30 minutes or until heated through. Or reheat in the microwave.

ROAST LAMB WITH GARLIC ROSEMARY SAUCE

MAKES 8 SERVINGS

I tasted this recipe at the first Sephardic Seder I attended. The shoulder cut is used in this recipe because the hind quarter of the lamb is not kosher. Personally, I think the shoulder has more flavor than the leg. Ask your butcher to bone the roast, roll, and tie it. Never cook lamb well-done; the interior should always be slightly pink.

One 5- to 7-pound boneless lamb shoulder roast

3 large cloves garlic, slivered

1 tablespoon fresh rosemary leaves,
    or 1 teaspoon dried

1/2 cup semidry white wine

1 tablespoon coarsely ground black pepper

1/4 teaspoon salt

1 tablespoon olive oil

Zest of 1 lemon, cut into slivers

2 teaspoons potato starch

Lemon slices, for garnish

1. Preheat the oven to 350°F. Wipe the lamb all over with a damp paper towel. With the tip of a sharp knife, make about 8 slashes in the skin approximately 1 inch deep. Insert half of the garlic slivers and half of the rosemary leaves into the slashes. In a small bowl, combine the white wine with the remaining garlic and rosemary, then stir in the pepper, salt, and oil.

2. Place the roast in a 15 1/2 × 13 1/2-inch roasting pan. Pour the wine mixture all over the lamb.

3. Roast, uncovered, allowing about 20 minutes to the pound, or 1 1/2 to 2 hours. Baste the roast occasionally with the pan drippings.

4. Scatter the slivers of lemon zest over the shoulder and continue to roast 30 minutes more. The meat should be well browned, and the interior slightly pink.

5. Remove the meat from the pan to a serving platter. Pour the contents left in the pan into a degreaser container if you have one or allow the liquid to stand for a few minutes to give the fat a chance to float to the top, then place paper towels on top to soak up as much grease as possible.

6. Place the liquid in a food processor or blender, add the potato starch, and process or blend until a smooth gravy has formed. Slice the lamb, arrange on a warm platter, and garnish with slices of lemon. Pass the gravy in a heated gravy boat.

SCALLOPED ORANGE ROUGHY

MAKES 8 SERVINGS

Cod, sole, or other small fish fillets can be substituted for the orange roughy. The soup nuts,
or *mandlen,* look like miniature puff pastry balls.
You can find them in the kosher food section at
your supermarket or deli. During Passover, I grind
the *mandlen* and use them in place of bread
crumbs. They're also a great addition, whole, to
any clear broth instead of matzo balls. I guess that's
how they got the name "soup nuts."

*8 medium fresh orange roughy fillets
    (3 to 4 pounds total)*

One 1³/4-ounce box soup nuts (mandlen), *ground*

¹/2 cup finely ground farfel

Salt and freshly ground black pepper to taste

*1 tablespoon chopped fresh basil,
    or 1 teaspoon dried*

3 tablespoons butter or margarine, melted

1 tablespoon grated mozzarella cheese (optional)

One 15-ounce jar marinara sauce

Microwave Method

1. Place the fish fillets in a 9×13-inch
microwave-safe casserole, with their thickest end
toward the outside edges of the dish. Cover with a
damp paper towel.

2. Microwave on high for 5 to 8 minutes, rotat-
ing the dish after 4 minutes. Remove the casserole
from the microwave oven and let stand, covered
with the damp paper towel, while preparing the
crumb mixture.

3. In a small bowl, use a fork to mix the ground
mandlen, ground farfel, salt, pepper, basil, and
melted butter.

4. Remove the paper towel from fish and drain
off any liquid that may have accumulated. Sprinkle
evenly with the cheese, if desired, then the crumb
mixture. Pour the marinara sauce on top, spreading
it evenly over the surface of the fish. Microwave on
high for 4 to 6 minutes or until the fish flakes when
tested with a fork. Serve.

Conventional Method

The fish can be baked in a large, lightly greased
casserole, covered with aluminum foil, in a 400°F
oven. Continue with steps 2 and 3 above, then finish baking in the oven for 10 to 12 minutes.

STUFFED WHITEFISH WITH WHITE WINE

MAKES 6 TO 8 SERVINGS

An easy method of knowing how long to bake fresh fish is to measure the fish at its thickest point and allow 10 minutes for each inch of thickness. Have fish filleted and butterflied at the store.

FISH AND STUFFING

One 3- to 4-pound fresh whole whitefish, boned and butterflied
1 teaspoon freshly squeezed lemon juice
1/4 cup white wine
1 teaspoon olive oil
1 small green bell pepper, coarsely chopped
8 ounces mushrooms, thinly sliced
1/4 cup finely chopped fresh parsley
2 green onions, thinly sliced
1 rib celery, thinly sliced
6 tablespoons (3/4 stick) butter or margarine
2 medium tomatoes, seeded and chopped
1/4 cup farfel
1/4 teaspoon chopped fresh oregano
Salt and freshly ground black pepper to taste

WHITE WINE SAUCE

1/4 cup white wine
1 tablespoon freshly squeezed lemon juice
2 teaspoons butter
2 teaspoons olive oil
1 teaspoon potato starch
1 tablespoon chopped fresh rosemary
Pinch of cayenne pepper

Preparing and Stuffing the Fish

1. Preheat the oven to 400°F. Wipe the fish inside and out with paper towels. In a 1-cup measure, combine the lemon juice, wine, and olive oil. Brush the fish inside and out with this mixture and set aside. Pour any remaining liquid into an 18×24-inch baking pan.

2. In a large bowl, mix the green pepper, mushrooms, parsley, green onions, and celery. Heat the butter in a large nonstick skillet over medium-high heat. When it begins to bubble, add the chopped vegetables. Reduce the heat to medium and cook, stirring often, for 5 to 6 minutes. Add the chopped tomato and cook 1 to 2 minutes longer. Remove from the heat.

3. Fold in the farfel and oregano. Season with salt and pepper and mix the stuffing ingredients well. With the fish open before you, spoon the stuffing down one side of the fish cavity. Fold the

other side of the fish over the stuffing and secure the sides together with toothpicks. Place the fish in the prepared baking dish.

4. Bake for about 35 minutes. Remove the fish from the oven and place on a serving platter. Cover with heavy aluminum foil to keep it warm while preparing the wine sauce.

Preparing the Wine Sauce

Add the white wine, lemon juice, butter, and oil to the fish pan. Scrape the pan and empty the contents into a processor or blender. Add the potato starch, rosemary, and cayenne pepper and process or blend until well mixed. Pour over the top of the fish and serve.

SCARLET CHICKEN

MAKES 8 SERVINGS

Dried cranberries and dried cherries are no longer considered gourmet. The addition of these dried fruits gives a distinctive flavor to the sauce. This recipe freezes well and can be prepared 3 days ahead. If you wish, you can mix chicken breasts and thighs if some of your family likes dark meat.

1/2 cup dried Bing cherries
1/2 cup dried cranberries
6 whole chicken breasts, cut in half
1 1/2 cups store-bought orange juice
1/2 cup sherry
1/2 cup brown sugar
3 teaspoons potato starch

1. Preheat the oven to 350°F. Place the dried fruit in a medium bowl filled with hot water and let stand for 10 to 15 minutes. Drain and set aside.

2. Lay the chicken pieces, skin side up, in an oblong baking pan. In a medium bowl, combine the orange juice, sherry, and brown sugar. Mix well, then stir in the dried cherries and cranberries and potato starch. Stir together, making sure the potato starch is dissolved.

3. Pour the sauce over the chicken pieces and bake, uncovered, for 45 minutes. Baste and bake 30 to 40 more minutes, covering the baking pan with aluminum foil during the last 15 minutes. The chicken should look a little crispy on top, and the sauce should begin to thicken. If the sauce gets too thick, add about 1/4 cup orange juice or water during the last 15 minutes of baking.

Turkey Scaloppini with Marinated Tomatoes

Makes 8 servings

Your guests will think they're eating veal because after the turkey cutlets are completed, they taste similar to veal. The marinated tomatoes can be prepared a day ahead, and the turkey scallops breaded and refrigerated earlier in the day.

MARINATED TOMATOES

6 cups cherry tomatoes
(three 12-ounce containers), cut in half

1 small red onion, thinly sliced

8 to 10 large fresh basil leaves, cut into thin strips

1/2 cup extra virgin olive oil

Freshly ground black pepper and salt to taste

TURKEY SCALLOPS

One 1 3/4-ounce box soup nuts (mandlen), ground

1/2 cup matzo cake meal

1 teaspoon dried basil

1/2 teaspoon dried oregano

2 large eggs or 1/2 cup egg substitute

2 tablespoons water

Salt and freshly ground black pepper to taste

2 pounds turkey cutlets (approximately 12 pieces)

3 tablespoons margarine

3 tablespoons olive oil

1. To make the marinated tomatoes, place the cherry tomatoes in a large bowl. In a 4-cup measure, mix the onion, basil, olive oil, and pepper together. Pour over the cherry tomatoes. Stir lightly to combine. Cover and refrigerate. Serve at room temperature or heat in microwave until slightly warmed just before serving the dish. Season with salt.

2. To make the turkey scallops, place the ground soup nuts on a sheet of waxed paper. In a small bowl, mix the matzo cake meal, basil, and oregano together. Empty onto another sheet of waxed paper. In a 2-cup measure, lightly beat the eggs together with the water and empty into a large pie plate.

3. Salt and pepper each turkey cutlet. Dredge each cutlet in the matzo cake meal mixture first, then the egg, then the soup nut crumbs. Place on a platter or baking sheet in single layers, separating the layers with waxed paper. Refrigerate for 2 to 3 hours.

4. Place half the margarine and oil in a large skillet over medium-high heat. Add the cutlets and brown for 2 to 3 minutes on each side. After you have cooked half the turkey cutlets, remove the pan from the heat, and wipe the pan out.

5. Return the pan to the heat; add the remaining oil and margarine, and repeat the process. Keep the cutlets warm, but serve as soon as possible. Top each serving with several tablespoons of marinated cherry tomatoes.

VEGETARIAN ROAST

MAKES 6 SERVINGS

Miriam Peerless was my Young Judea leader when I was in high school. We have remained friends over the years. She developed this recipe for one of her sons, who is a vegetarian. This is her Passover version.

1/4 cup margarine

1 large onion, chopped

5 large eggs, well beaten,
   or 11/4 cups egg substitute

2 teaspoons pareve chicken soup granules

4 cups small-curd cottage cheese

1 cup toasted walnuts, finely chopped
   (see La Salada Vert, page 53, to toast walnuts)

3 cups farfel

1. In a large skillet, melt the margarine over medium heat. Add the onion and cook, stirring, until wilted. Add the remaining ingredients and cook 2 to 3 more minutes, stirring well.

2. Preheat the oven to 350°F. Place the onion mixture in a greased 9×13-inch baking pan. Bake for 45 to 60 minutes. Let cool, then remove from the pan. Slice and serve with a mushroom or fresh tomato sauce, if desired.

APPLE MATZO KUGEL

MAKES 8 TO 10 SERVINGS

With the addition of cinnamon and cumin, this traditional Seder recipe takes on a Moroccan flavor. It can be prepared weeks ahead. Slice the kugel into serving pieces, place them in a microwave-safe casserole, wrap well in heavy aluminum foil, and freeze. When ready to serve, remove the foil and reheat the kugel in your microwave.

4 matzos

1 cup chicken stock

2 large eggs

2 large egg whites

3 tablespoons margarine, melted

1/4 teaspoon salt

1/2 teaspoon ground cumin

1 teaspoon ground cinnamon

2 large tart apples, peeled, cored, and sliced

1 cup chopped walnuts

1 cup golden raisins

1. Preheat the oven to 350°F. Grease a 9-inch square glass baking pan. In a medium bowl, break the matzos into small pieces and soak them in the chicken stock until softened, about 5 minutes.

2. In a large bowl, combine the eggs, egg whites, 2 tablespoons of the melted margarine, and the salt, cumin, and cinnamon. Beat with a wire whisk and pour over the matzos.

3. Stir in the apples, walnuts, and raisins. Spoon the mixture into the prepared pan and drizzle the remaining 1 tablespoon of margarine over the top. Bake for 30 to 40 minutes or until slightly browned. Serve warm.

CARROT-YAM TZIMMES

MAKES 6 TO 8 SERVINGS

The secret to this traditional dish is its slow baking. Each time I've prepared it, everyone raves about its fantastic flavor and unusual consistency. It's great with any poultry or roast. If you wish to freeze the *tzimmes*, let it cool a little before placing it in the freezer.

3 cups sliced cooked carrots

1/3 cup orange juice

1/4 cup sherry

One 17-ounce can sweet potatoes, sliced

1/3 cup honey

1/2 cup pineapple preserves

8 pitted prunes, quartered

8 dried apricots, quartered

1/4 teaspoon ground ginger

1 tablespoon sugar

1/8 teaspoon ground cinnamon

Pinch of salt

1. Preheat the oven to 300°F. Drain the carrots and place them in a large bowl. Add the remaining ingredients. Gently mix everything together.

2. Transfer to a greased 2-quart casserole. Bake, covered, for 2 1/2 to 3 hours, until heated through. Serve warm.

HANNA BEAR'S LEVIVOT

(CAULIFLOWER FRITTERS)

MAKES 20 SMALL FRITTERS

Last year our daughter Karen's mother-in-law, Hanna Bear, visited us from Israel. We all raved about these cauliflower fritters. Her method was traditional, but the concept and flavor were new to us all.

1 medium head cauliflower

3 large eggs

1 clove garlic, minced

1/2 cup matzo cake meal

3/4 teaspoon salt

Freshly ground black pepper to taste

1/4 teaspoon ground cinnamon

1 teaspoon ground cumin

1/2 teaspoon turmeric

Oil for frying

1. Remove the core and most of stem portion from the cauliflower and break into florets. Place in a steaming basket, set in a saucepan with 1 inch of water, cover, and steam for 4 to 6 minutes or until tender. Drain well and place in a large bowl. Mash with a fork. Add the eggs, garlic, matzo cake meal, salt, pepper, cinnamon, cumin, and turmeric. Mix together well.

2. Heat 3 to 4 tablespoons of oil in a large skillet. Use a large soup spoon to drop the cauliflower batter into the skillet, making small pancakes.

3. Flatten each pancake slightly with the back of the spoon. Fry for 2 to 3 minutes on each side or until light brown. Add more oil to the skillet if necessary. Drain on paper towels. Serve warm. These can be frozen.

MACARONI AND CHEESE PASSOVER STYLE

MAKES 6 TO 8 SERVINGS

Adults and children will love this dish. Farfel is not macaroni, but it makes a delightful and welcome replacement for pasta during Passover week.

3 large eggs

3¹/2 cups farfel, or 6 whole matzos broken into small pieces

1 cup milk

1 teaspoon salt

¹/4 teaspoon ground white pepper

8 ounces cheddar cheese, cut into 2-inch pieces

1 pint sour cream

4 ounces (1 stick) butter, cut into 16 pieces

1. Preheat the oven 350°F. In a medium bowl, lightly beat 2 of the eggs and mix in the farfel or broken matzos.

2. In a 4-cup measure or blender, beat the remaining egg with the milk, salt, and pepper.

3. Grease or spray a 2-quart rectangular casserole. Place half of the farfel mixture and half of the cheese in the casserole. Add half of the sour cream, distributing it in dollops evenly on the surface, then half of the butter pieces. Make a second layer in the same fashion. Pour the milk mixture on top.

4. Cover the casserole and bake for 30 minutes. Uncover and bake 10 to 15 minutes longer to brown the top. Cut into squares and serve.

YELENA RURA'S MUSHROOMS JULIENNE

MAKES 6 TO 8 SERVINGS

My Russian friend Yelena Rura served this at her grandson Shimon's *bris*. I enjoy preparing this casserole, especially when I have guests who are vegetarians.

2 tablespoons butter or margarine

1 pound fresh mushrooms, sliced

3 medium onions, sliced

2 large carrots, sliced

1 1/2 teaspoons potato starch

*Salt and freshly ground black
    pepper to taste*

1 cup sour cream

1/2 cup grated medium-sharp cheese

1. In a medium skillet, melt 1 tablespoon of the butter or margarine over medium-high heat. Add the mushrooms and sauté for 4 to 5 minutes, or until the mushrooms release their juices and look slightly golden in color. Remove with a slotted spoon to a bowl.

2. Add the remaining tablespoon of butter or margarine to the skillet and sauté the onions and carrots until the onions begin to turn golden brown, about 5 minutes.

3. Preheat the broiler. Return the mushrooms to the skillet and continue to cook the vegetables for 1 to 2 more minutes, stirring. Add the potato starch, salt, pepper, and sour cream. Mix well.

4. Transfer the vegetable mixture to a 1-quart flameproof casserole. Sprinkle the grated cheese evenly over the top. Broil the mushroom casserole just until the cheese melts, 1 to 2 minutes. Serve warm.

*Note: The casserole can be refrigerated after the
    cheese is sprinkled on top. When ready to
    serve, place it under the broiler to melt the
    cheese. This recipe is easily doubled or
    tripled.*

RHUBARB COMPOTE

MAKES 6 TO 8 SERVINGS

Rhubarb is a favorite of mine. I love it in pie or stewed. The addition of apples and strawberries gives this compote a flavor and texture that create a beautiful, light, and satisfying side dish with lamb or dessert. The almond extract and cardamom take away the "bite."

1 pound rhubarb, cut into 1-inch pieces
1 pound tart apples, peeled, cored,
   and cut into 1-inch pieces
1/2 pint strawberries, stemmed and left whole
1/2 to 1 cup sugar
Pinch of ground cardamom
1/8 teaspoon almond extract

Microwave Method

Place the rhubarb, apples, and strawberries in a 3-quart microwave-safe bowl. Add the remaining ingredients and stir well. Cover the bowl with vented plastic wrap and microwave on high for 10 minutes. Serve at room temperature. This will thicken as it cools.

Conventional Method

Place the rhubarb, apples, and strawberries in a large nonreactive saucepan. Add the sugar, cardamom, and almond extract. Cover. Over medium-high heat, bring the fruit to a slow boil. Reduce the heat to low and simmer, uncovered, for 10 to 15 minutes or until fruit is soft. Serve at room temperature. This will thicken as it cools.

Ruth's Matzo Farfel Dressing

Makes 8 to 10 servings

This is the most frequently requested dish at Ruth Pleatman's annual Seder dinners. Ruth says the inspiration for it came from combining many grandmothers' best recipes. It is so delicious that there's no need to stuff the dressing inside a turkey or chicken. It's versatile and can star as a vegetarian entrée. Ruth often chops the onions, celery, green pepper, mushrooms, and parsley a day in advance to save time.

1 pound farfel

3 cups pareve chicken stock or broth

8 ounces (2 sticks) butter or margarine

1 cup chopped onion

1 cup chopped celery

1/4 cup chopped green bell pepper (optional)

2 cups sliced mushrooms

2 tablespoons chopped fresh parsley

1 large clove garlic, minced

1 medium apple, peeled and grated

2 large eggs, beaten

1 teaspoon ground ginger

1 teaspoon salt

1/4 teaspoon freshly ground black pepper

1. Preheat the oven to 350°F. Place the farfel in a large bowl; add the chicken stock and let stand for 15 minutes.

2. Meanwhile, melt the butter or margarine in a large skillet over medium-high heat. Add the onion, celery, bell pepper, if desired, mushrooms, and parsley and sauté until the onion is golden, about 5 minutes. Mix in the garlic and grated apple.

3. Stir the sautéed mixture into the softened farfel and let cool. Add the eggs, ginger, salt, and pepper and mix until well combined. Spoon the mixture into a greased 9×13-inch casserole.

4. Bake for 30 minutes; remove from the oven. Turn the dressing over with a spoon, breaking it up in order to brown the other side. Bake an additional 30 minutes or until golden brown.

Note: This recipe can be prepared in advance (including baking) and then frozen.

LESHA'S THREE-VEGETABLE GATEAU

MAKES 8 TO 10 SERVINGS

This absolutely smashing vegetarian entrée can be prepared 1 or 2 days ahead. Although it takes a little time, its flavor and presentation will win everyone over.

My Cincinnati friend Lesha Greengus and her husband, Sam, who is a professor of Semitic Languages at the Cincinnati Hebrew Union College Jewish Institute of Religion, are always entertaining guest speakers and visiting professors. "They rave about it," she said. "I never have any left over. I created this recipe to please my children, who are vegetarians."

Each vegetable is cooked separately, then layered in a loaf pan. The vegetables can be cooked and refrigerated a day or two before you assemble them in the loaf pan. I use kosher for Passover olive oil spray to grease the pan and waxed paper.

1 pound cauliflower florets

1 1/2 pounds Idaho potatoes, peeled and quartered

1 pound carrots, sliced

1 pound sweet potatoes, peeled and sliced

1 cup store-bought orange juice

12 ounces broccoli florets

1 tablespoon olive oil

1 tablespoon margarine

1 medium onion, thinly sliced

1 large clove garlic, chopped

1 teaspoon ground cumin

1/4 teaspoon turmeric

2 1/2 tablespoons matzo cake meal

2 1/2 tablespoons potato starch

1 1/2 cups egg substitute

Salt and freshly ground black pepper to taste

1/2 teaspoon freshly grated or ground nutmeg

1/2 teaspoon ground cinnamon

1/4 teaspoon ground cardamom

2 tablespoons brown sugar

1. Place cauliflower in a large microwave-safe bowl. Microwave on high for 6 to 8 minutes, or until tender. Drain, cover, and refrigerate.

2. In a large saucepan, cover the white potatoes with water and cook for 15 minutes over medium-high heat, or until tender. Drain, cover, and refrigerate.

3. Place the carrots and sweet potatoes in a large saucepan. Add the orange juice and 1 cup water; bring to a boil. Reduce heat and simmer for 10 minutes or until tender. Drain, cover, and refrigerate.

4. Place the broccoli in a microwave-safe container. Microwave on high for 6 minutes or until tender. Drain, cover, and refrigerate.

5. To make the gateau, in a medium skillet, heat the olive oil and margarine over medium-high heat. Add the onion and garlic and sauté until the onion is transparent. Remove from the pan and set aside.

6. Grease a $9 \times 5^{1}/_{2} \times 3$-inch glass loaf pan. (I prefer glass because you can see each layer.) Line the bottom with waxed paper and grease the paper.

7. To make the cauliflower layer, place the cauliflower in a food processor and pulse several times. Add half of the cooked white potatoes and pulse several more times. Add half of the sautéed onion-garlic mixture and the cumin, turmeric, $^1/_2$ tablespoon of cake meal, and $^1/_2$ tablespoon of the potato starch. Pulse several times.

8. With the processor running, pour $^1/_2$ cup of the egg substitute through the feed tube. Process for 1 minute, stopping to scrape down the sides of the bowl now and then. Pulse and process until the mixture is smooth. Add salt and pepper to taste. Pulse several times.

9. Place the mixture in the prepared loaf pan. It should fill about $^1/_3$ of the pan. Smooth the top evenly. (Should you have any left over, place it in a smaller greased loaf pan or casserole.)

10. To make the carrot–sweet potato layer, remove the cutting blade and wipe out the processor bowl. Replace the blade and add the cooked carrots and sweet potatoes. Pulse several times. Add the nutmeg, cinnamon, cardamom, and brown sugar. Pulse several more times.

11. With the processor running, pour $^1/_2$ cup of the egg substitute through the feed tube. Process for 1 minute. Add 1 tablespoon of the matzo cake meal and 1 tablespoon of the potato starch. Pulse and process until the mixture is smooth.

12. Place the carrot–sweet potato mixture directly on top of the cauliflower. Smooth the top evenly. (Should you have any left over, place it on top of the cauliflower in the second pan or casserole.)

13. To make the broccoli layer, remove the cutting blade and wipe out the processor bowl. Replace the blade and add the cooked broccoli with the remaining cooked potatoes and the remaining onion-garlic mixture. Pulse several times, stopping to scrape down the sides of the bowl now and then.

14. With the processor running, pour the remaining $^1/_2$ cup egg substitute through the feed tube. Process for 1 minute. Add the remaining 1 tablespoon of matzo cake meal and remaining 1 tablespoon potato starch, and salt and pepper to taste. Pulse and process until the mixture is smooth.

continues

15. Spoon the broccoli mixture into the prepared loaf pan directly on top of the carrot mixture. Smooth the top evenly. (Should you have any left over, place it on top of the carrots in the second pan or casserole.) The gateau can be covered and refrigerated for 1 or 2 days before baking.

16. Preheat the oven to 375°F. Set the prepared loaf pan (and the second pan if you have one) into the center of a larger pan that can hold a water bath. Set on the center of the rack in the lower third of the preheated oven. Pour hot water into the larger pan to come halfway up the sides of the loaf pan. Cover the gateau lightly with aluminum foil and bake for about 1 hour 15 minutes or until the tip of a knife placed in the center comes out clean.

17. Remove the loaf pan from the water bath. Allow it to rest for 10 to 15 minutes. Cover and refrigerate at least 2 hours. When ready to serve, slice the gateau. Place the slices in an ovenproof casserole and warm the slices, covered, in a 400°F oven for 10 minutes.

Variations

1. If you prefer not to make this as a loaf, you can bake each vegetable mixture separately in its own greased casserole in a water bath. When ready to serve, use an ice cream scoop to make vegetable balls on a large platter. You'll still have the three colors, but if someone prefers one vegetable over another, they have a choice.

2. Prepare only one of the vegetable mixtures and serve it as a side dish in the center of an acorn squash, orange shells, or bell peppers.

3. You may substitute spinach for the broccoli, or turnips and parsnips for the cauliflower. You can substitute frozen cauliflower and broccoli but not frozen carrots. You can also use different herbs, such as dill with the broccoli or cauliflower.

SPINACH-VEGETABLE SQUARES

MAKES 8 SERVINGS

This side dish can also be used as an alternative entrée for the vegetarian Seder menu.

3 large carrots

One 10-ounce package frozen spinach, thawed

1 medium onion, quartered

2 medium green bell peppers, diced

2 ribs celery, cut into 2-inch pieces

*1 pareve chicken bouillon cube
    mixed with 1 cup boiling water*

2 large eggs

3/4 cup matzo meal

1 teaspoon grated nutmeg

1/2 teaspoon freshly ground black pepper

Processor Method

1. Preheat the oven to 350°F. Spray an 8-inch square pan with vegetable spray. Cut carrots to fit the feed tube of your food processor. Insert the grater disc and, using medium pressure, grate the carrots; set aside.

2. Remove grater disc from the processor and insert the steel blade. Place the spinach, onion, bell peppers, and celery in the processor and pulse several times. Scrape the bowl and pulse until vegetables are finely chopped.

3. Empty into a large saucepan. Add the grated carrots and prepared chicken bouillon. Cook, uncovered, over medium heat 15 to 20 minutes, or until the vegetables are soft and the liquid is reduced to 1/4 cup.

4. Place the eggs, matzo meal, nutmeg, and pepper in the processor. Process for 30 seconds, then fold into the cooked vegetables. Spread evenly in the prepared pan. Bake, uncovered, for 45 minutes. Cut into squares and serve.

Conventional Method
Chop and grate the vegetables by hand. Cook as directed in step 3 above. In step 4, use a rotary or portable electric mixer to beat the egg mixture. Continue as directed above.

TOMATO SLICES PROVENÇAL

MAKES 4 SERVINGS

Everyone seems to love these tomatoes. They can be baked in the morning, then refrigerated and finished just before serving. The recipe can easily be doubled. For a dairy meal you can add ¼ cup grated Parmesan cheese to the crumb mixture.

2 firm, ripe tomatoes (about 3 inches in diameter)
Salt and freshly ground black pepper to taste
1 cup finely ground soup nuts (mandlen)
3 tablespoons oil
1 clove garlic, minced
4 thin slices red onion
1 tablespoon chopped fresh basil

1. Preheat the oven to 350°F. Slice the stem and a small piece from the other side of the tomatoes and discard. Cut the tomatoes into 1-inch slices. You should get at least 2 thick slices from each tomato. Place the slices in a medium baking dish. Season with salt and pepper.

2. In a small bowl, combine the soup nut crumbs, oil, and garlic. Spread evenly onto each tomato slice. Top with a slice of onion.

3. Sprinkle evenly with the basil. Bake, uncovered, for 15 minutes, or microwave on high, covered loosely, until heated through, 2 to 3 minutes. Remove the cover after a minute.

ZUCCHINI AU GRATIN

MAKES 4 TO 6 SERVINGS

This year it seems more cooking magazines have featured gratin dishes than ever before. Maybe because they're the perfect answer when last-minute guests appear, since they're easy, quick, and lovely looking.

1 tablespoon butter

1 cup sliced mushrooms

2 shallots, sliced

1 1/2 pounds zucchini, thinly sliced

3/4 cup light cream

3 large egg yolks

Salt and freshly ground black pepper to taste

Pinch of curry powder

1/4 cup grated sharp cheese

1. In a small skillet, melt the butter over medium-high heat. Add the mushrooms and shallots and sauté until the mushrooms release their juices, about 5 minutes. Set aside.

2. Place the zucchini in a medium saucepan and cover with cold water. Bring to a boil and blanch them no more than 2 to 3 minutes. Drain and mix with the sautéed vegetables. Spread in a 9×13-inch baking dish.

3. In a medium bowl, whisk the cream and egg yolks together. Add the salt, pepper, and curry powder and mix until well blended. Pour over the vegetables. Sprinkle the cheese evenly over the top. (You can prepare the recipe up to this point 1 day ahead, cover, and refrigerate.)

4. Preheat the oven to 350°F. Bake the zucchini for 30 to 45 minutes or until golden brown on top.

Assorted Muffins

Makes 12 muffins

This is a basic recipe for Passover muffins. These can be prepared sweet or savory, depending on the additional ingredients you include. They're great for meals as well as snacks.

1/4 cup matzo cake meal

1/4 cup potato starch

2 tablespoons sugar

1/4 teaspoon salt

3 large eggs

1/2 cup vegetable oil

1. Preheat the oven to 325°F. Grease or place paper liners in a muffin pan.

2. In a 2-quart bowl, sift the matzo cake meal, potato starch, sugar, and salt together.

3. In a small bowl, beat the eggs and oil together. Add this to the dry ingredients. Add and fold in any additional ingredients at this point (see Variations). Stir lightly.

4. Spoon the batter into the prepared muffin pan, filling the cups about 2/3 full. Sprinkle muffin tops with your choice of topping. Bake for 25 to 30 minutes or until the muffins are brown.

Variations

For sweet muffins, in step 3, add 1/2 cup sugar plus one or more of the following:

1 teaspoon nutmeg, cinnamon, or ginger

1/2 cup dried raisins, apricots, figs, dates, pears, chopped peaches, or cranberries

3/4 cup chopped pecans, almonds, walnuts, or hazelnuts

For savory muffins, in step 3, add one or more of the following:

1 teaspoon minced garlic or onion

1 teaspoon fresh chopped fresh basil, thyme, oregano, or rosemary

1/4 cup grated sharp cheese

Choose one of the following toppings for sweet or savory muffins:

1 tablespoon cinnamon sugar

1 tablespoon grated chocolate

1 tablespoon chopped fresh herbs

1 tablespoon finely chopped nuts

1 tablespoon paprika

PASSOVER BANANA "BREAD"

MAKES 2 LOAVES

The kids will love this. Slice it for dessert and serve with homemade applesauce.

5 large eggs, separated

3/4 cup sugar

1/4 cup matzo cake meal

1 tablespoon potato starch

1 large banana, cut into thirds

1 tablespoon freshly squeezed orange juice

1 tablespoon grated orange zest

1/2 cup golden raisins, soaked in hot water and drained

Processor Method

1. Preheat the oven to 325°F. Grease or spray two 7 7/8 × 3 7/8-inch aluminum foil loaf pans.

2. Place the egg yolks and sugar in a food processor and process for 1 minute or until thick and pale yellow.

3. Sift the matzo cake meal and potato starch together and add to the processor along with the banana and orange juice and zest. Process until you can no longer see the banana. Remove to a large bowl and fold in the raisins.

4. In a separate large bowl, beat the egg whites until stiff peaks form. Fold into the batter. Pour into the prepared pans. Bake for 1 hour or until a toothpick inserted in center of loaf comes out clean. Let cool completely before removing from the pans.

Conventional Method

Follow step 1 above. Then use an electric mixer to beat the egg yolks, sugar, banana, and orange juice and zest. Add the sifted dry ingredients, mix well, and proceed to step 4 above.

GARLIC "BREAD"

MAKES 1 LOAF

It's amazing what you can do with matzo meal and eggs. This garlic "bread" won't last long once it comes out of the oven.

1/2 cup vegetable oil

2 tablespoons olive oil

1 cup cold water

1 cup matzo meal

1 teaspoon salt

1 teaspoon chopped fresh basil

4 large eggs

2 large cloves garlic

Processor Method

1. Combine the vegetable oil with 1 tablespoon of the olive oil and the water in a small saucepan and bring to a boil. Remove the pan from the heat and add the matzo meal, salt, and basil. Stir well with a wooden spoon.

2. Preheat the oven to 375°F. Place the matzo meal mixture and eggs in a food processor fitted with a metal blade and pulse several times to blend. With the machine running, drop 1 clove of the garlic through the feed tube. Process until the mixture begins to form a ball around the metal blade.

3. Remove the dough from the processor. Dip you hands in a little matzo cake meal and shape the dough into an oval loaf.

4. Place on an ungreased cookie sheet and bake for 40 to 50 minutes or until the top is golden brown. Remove from the baking sheet and let cool for 10 minutes on a wire rack. Split the loaf in half horizontally.

5. Preheat the broiler. Mince the remaining clove of garlic and mix with the remaining tablespoon of olive oil. Spread over each half loaf. Toast the "bread" under the broiler just until it begins to turn slightly golden in color. Cut into slices and serve immediately.

Conventional Method

In step 2 above, chop the garlic fine. Mix the eggs and half of the garlic into the matzo-meal mixture with a fork or an electric mixer. Remove the dough from the bowl. Dip your hands into a little matzo cake meal and shape the dough into an oval loaf. Continue as in step 4 and 5 of processor method.

Variation: Herbed Matzo Puffs

You will need 3 tablespoons of mixed dried herbs, such as oregano, rosemary, thyme, or chives. In step 2, mix 2 tablespoons of the mixed herbs into the dough. Shape the dough into balls the size of a muffin. In step 5, split the puffs in half and brush the insides with a little oil mixed with the other tablespoon of herbs.

JUDY'S MATZO BAGELS

MAKES 12 TO 14 BAGELS

Judy Simon was a member of my focus group and one of the recipe testers. Her input was invaluable. Since we can't have bread for Passover, these bagels are standard fare and are great for making sandwiches for school lunches. I bake several batches and freeze them. I like adding a little sugar; Judy prefers hers without.

1 cup water

1/2 cup vegetable oil

2 cups matzo meal

4 large eggs

1 teaspoon salt

1/2 teaspoon sugar (optional)

1. In a medium saucepan over medium-high heat, boil the water and oil together. Add the matzo meal all at once, stirring with a wooden spoon until the mixture begins to pull away from the sides of the pan. Remove from the heat and allow to cool for 15 minutes.

2. Add 2 eggs at a time, beating well after each addition. Add the salt and, if desired, the sugar. Wet your hands with cold water or grease them with a little oil, and form the dough into balls the size of a large egg.

3. Preheat the oven to 350°F. Place the balls on a baking sheet and poke a hole in the center using the end of the handle of a wooden spoon. Bake for 45 to 50 minutes.

ONION ROLLS FOR PASSOVER

MAKES 12 ROLLS

These can be split and used as a base for tuna, chicken, or egg salad sandwiches. The dough can be made ahead, refrigerated overnight, and baked the next morning.

1 small onion, cut in half

1 tablespoon chicken fat (schmaltz) *or margarine*

1/2 cup oil

1 cup cold water

1 cup matzo meal

1 1/2 to 2 teaspoons salt

4 large eggs

1 egg for egg wash (optional)

Processor Method

1. Preheat the oven to 350°F. Insert the metal blade in a food processor. With the machine running, drop the onion into the feed tube and process until minced.

2. In a small skillet over medium-high heat, melt the chicken fat or margarine. Add the onion and sauté until golden brown. Set aside.

3. Over high heat, bring the oil and water to a boil in a large saucepan. Remove from the heat and add the matzo meal and 1 1/2 teaspoons of the salt all at once. Mix well with a wooden spoon.

4. Place the mixture in a food processor, add 2 of the eggs, and pulse once or twice. Add the remaining 2 eggs and the sautéed onion. Pulse until well mixed. Remove to a mixing bowl.

5. Dipping your hands in the cold water, shape the dough into 2-inch rolls and place about 2 inches apart on a greased cookie sheet. If using the egg wash, combine the egg and the remaining 1/2 teaspoon salt in a small bowl and brush this on the tops of the rolls. Bake for 50 to 60 minutes or until golden brown. Let cool for several minutes before removing from the baking sheet.

Conventional Method

Follow the steps above, but in step 2, mince the onion with a knife, and in step 5, use an electric mixer instead of a food processor.

APPLES WITH MERINGUE TOPPING

MAKES 6 SERVINGS

This dessert is simple to make yet elegant enough for the fanciest dinner party. You can prepare the apples earlier in the day, refrigerate them, and finish baking the meringue right before serving.

4 pounds Gala or Granny Smith apples

3/4 cup red cherry preserves

5 large egg whites

1 1/2 tablespoons confectioners' sugar

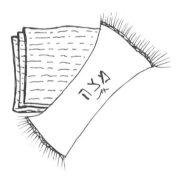

1. Peel, core, and quarter the apples. Place them in a large saucepan with 1/3 cup water. Cover and bring to a boil. Reduce the heat and simmer just until tender, about 15 minutes. Remove with a slotted spoon and transfer to a medium baking dish or soufflé dish.

2. Puree the preserves in a blender or food processor, spoon into a small bowl, and stir with a fork or small wire whisk. Spread evenly over the top of the apples.

3. Preheat the oven to 425°F. With an electric mixer, beat the egg whites in a large mixing bowl until foamy. Gradually add the sugar, beating constantly until stiff peaks form. Spoon the meringue lightly over the preserves, making sure it touches the rim of the dish so that everything is sealed inside. You can prepare the dessert to this point and refrigerate it until right before you're ready to bake and serve it. Bake for 7 to 10 minutes or until the meringue is lightly browned. Serve immediately.

APRICOT FREEZE

MAKES 6 SERVINGS

This is a little like sorbet but much easier to prepare.

One 24-ounce can pears, drained
1 tablespoon apricot preserves
1 teaspoon brandy or apricot liqueur
Fresh mint leaves for garnish

1. Place the pears in a single layer on a cookie sheet and freeze until hard, about 1 hour.

2. Remove from the freezer and place in a blender or food processor. Add the preserves and liqueur. Process or blend until smooth. Empty into a large metal bowl. Cover with plastic wrap and freeze for 1 to 1 1/2 hours. Scoop into sherbet glasses and garnish with mint.

BRANDIED FRESH GRAPES

MAKES 12 TO 16 SERVINGS

This is one of my family's favorites. It's a great party dessert or can be spooned over day-old sponge cake.

3 pounds green seedless grapes
1/2 cup clover honey
3 tablespoons freshly squeezed lemon juice
1/2 cup brandy
Sour cream and brown sugar for garnish

1. Remove the grapes from their stems and place in a large serving bowl. In a 2-cup glass measure, combine the honey, lemon juice, and brandy. Pour over the grapes and stir well. Cover and refrigerate for 3 to 5 hours, stirring from bottom to top every hour.

2. To serve, top with sour cream and brown sugar. Or pass the toppings in small bowls and allow the guests to help themselves.

CARROT CAKE FOR PASSOVER
WITH CREAM CHEESE GLAZE

MAKES 10 TO 12 SERVINGS

Although the consistency is lighter than most carrot cakes, the flavor is outstanding. Use the cream cheese glaze only when serving a dairy meal.

3/4 *cup matzo cake meal*

3/4 *cup potato starch*

1/4 *teaspoon salt*

2 *teaspoons ground cinnamon*

9 *large eggs, separated, at room temperature*

1 1/2 *cups sugar*

1/2 *cup frozen orange juice concentrate, thawed*

1 *tablespoon grated orange zest*

About 2 medium carrots, shredded (1 cup)

1/2 *cup finely chopped walnuts*

1 *cup golden raisins*

CREAM CHEESE GLAZE

6 *ounces cream cheese, at room temperature*

2 *tablespoons whipping cream*

2 *teaspoons vanilla extract, or 3 packets*
vanilla sugar

1 *tablespoon sugar*

Walnut halves for garnish

1. Preheat the oven to 325°F.

2. Sift together the matzo cake meal, potato starch, salt, and cinnamon. Set aside.

3. Place the egg whites in the large bowl of an electric mixer. Beat until foamy. Gradually add 1/2 cup of the sugar and beat until stiff peaks form. Set aside.

4. Place the egg yolks in another large bowl and beat with the electric mixer until thick and lemon colored, about 5 minutes. Gradually add the remaining 1 cup of sugar. Beat 2 to 3 more minutes. Add the sifted dry ingredients and orange juice concentrate alternately, mixing only until well blended.

5. On low speed, add the orange zest, carrots, walnuts, and raisins. Gently fold in the egg white mixture. Do not overmix.

6. Pour the cake into the tube pan and bake for 50 to 60 minutes or until the cake is golden brown and springs back when touched lightly with your finger. Invert the pan onto a cake rack or neck of a bottle. Let cool completely before removing from the pan.

Glazing the Cake
In a small bowl or food processor, beat the cream cheese and cream until smooth. Add the vanilla and sugar and mix in well. Spread over the top of the cooled cake. Garnish with walnut halves.

CHEESECAKE EXTRAORDINAIRE

MAKES 12 TO 16 SERVINGS

This recipe originated in St. Louis, Missouri. It was our friend Bob Blatt's favorite dessert and his late mother's specialty. I adapted it for a party I gave during Passover.

CRUST

One 6-ounce box amaretto nut cookies, finely ground

6 tablespoons (3/4 stick) butter or margarine, melted

FILLING

Three 8-ounce packages cream cheese

1 cup plus 2 teaspoons sugar

2 cups milk, or 1 cup milk and 1 cup heavy cream

1 teaspoon vanilla extract

2 tablespoons matzo cake meal

4 large eggs, separated

1/4 teaspoon ground nutmeg

Making the Crust

Preheat the oven to 350°F. Grease a 9-inch spring-form pan. In a small bowl, mix the amaretto crumbs with the melted butter and press in the bottom of the pan. Bake for 10 minutes. Remove from the oven and let cool.

Making the Filling

1. Preheat the oven to 325°F. In a food processor, process the cream cheese and 1 cup of the sugar for 15 to 30 seconds. In a 4-cup glass measure, combine the milk, vanilla, matzo cake meal, and egg yolks.

2. Add half the milk mixture to the cream cheese. Pulse 3 times, then process for 10 seconds. Pour this mixture into a large bowl. Process the remaining milk mixture for 10 seconds; empty into the bowl and mix.

3. In a separate large bowl, beat the egg whites with an electric mixer. While beating, slowly add the remaining 2 teaspoons sugar. Beat the whites just until they begin to hold stiff peaks (not too stiff). Fold into the cream cheese mixture and pour into the crust. Sprinkle the top evenly with the nutmeg.

4. Bake for about 1 hour or until the tip of a knife inserted in the center comes out clean. Turn the oven off, open the oven door, and leave the cheesecake in the oven for 30 minutes. Remove the cake and let it cool completely on a wire rack. Cover lightly and refrigerate overnight.

Conventional Method

Make the crust as above. To make the filling, bring the cream cheese to room temperature, then beat in 1 cup of the sugar with an electric mixer. Combine the milk, vanilla, matzo cake meal, and egg yolks as in step 1 and beat into the cream cheese using the mixer. Proceed with steps 3 and 4.

GLAZED APPLE TART

MAKES 8 TO 10 SERVINGS

This dessert is a family favorite. I adapted the crust so it adheres to Passover restrictions. Apples are available year-round. With so many new varieties, you may wish to mix 2 or 3 kinds together for the filling.

PASTRY

5 tablespoons margarine or butter,
   cut into 1-inch pieces

3/4 cup matzo cake meal

2 tablespoons potato starch

3 tablespoons sugar

1 large egg yolk

1 teaspoon vanilla extract

2 tablespoons liquid nondairy creamer or milk

APPLE FILLING

1/4 cup plus 2 tablespoons sugar

2 tablespoons potato starch

Juice of 2 large lemons, divided

Juice of 1 orange

4 large cooking apples, peeled, cored,
   and cut into 1/4-inch-thick rings

1/2 cup apricot preserves

1/2 teaspoon grated orange zest

1/2 teaspoon grated lemon zest

1 tablespoon margarine or butter, melted

1. Preheat the oven to 425°F. Grease a 9-inch tart pan with a removable bottom. To make the pastry, place the butter, matzo cake meal, potato starch, and sugar in a food processor and pulse several times, until the mixture resembles coarse meal.

2. In a 1-cup measure, mix the egg yolk, vanilla and the nondairy creamer or milk. With the processor running, pour this through the feed tube, processing until the dough begins to form a ball around the metal blade. If the dough looks too dry, add more liquid. Press the dough over the bottom of the tart pan and 1 inch up the sides.

3. To make the filling, mix 1/4 cup of the sugar and the potato starch together in a small bowl. Set aside. In a 1-cup measure, combine 2 tablespoons of the lemon juice and all the orange juice. Set aside.

4. Sprinkle 2 tablespoons of the sugar mixture on top of the pastry. Arrange half of the apple rings on the bottom of the pastry and sprinkle them with 2 tablespoons of the juice mixture and 2 tablespoons of the sugar mixture.

5. Place the remaining apple slices in the pan and sprinkle with the remaining juice mixture and sugar mixture.

6. In a small bowl, mix the remaining lemon juice and 2 tablespoons sugar with the apricot preserves, citrus zests, and butter. Lightly brush half of

this mixture over the top layer of apple rings. Place in the oven and bake for 30 minutes or until the apples are tender. If the pastry begins to get too brown, cover loosely with aluminum foil. Bake 5 more minutes. Remove the tart from the oven.

7. Preheat the broiler. Brush the remaining preserves mixture on the top of the tart. Broil the tart 6 inches from the heat until the apples are glazed and brown around the edges, 20 to 30 seconds. Watch carefully, as the apples brown easily. Remove the tart from the oven and let cool for 20 to 30 minutes before removing the sides of the pan. Serve warm or cold with sweetened whipped cream if desired.

Note: This recipe also works well with sliced pears.

FROZEN AMARETTO TORTE

MAKES 10 TO 12 SERVINGS

This recipe is not for those watching their calories. A large variety of Passover cookies are available to use in baking. I grind the cookies and use them as a base when baking pie crusts or cakes. I also use the cookie crumbs as a garnish or add them to toppings over fruit. You'll get 1 to 1 1/2 cups of ground cookie crumbs from each 6-ounce box.

2 cups heavy cream, whipped

4 large egg yolks

3/4 cup brown sugar

1/2 cup finely chopped pecans

*Two 6-ounce boxes amaretto nut cookies,
    finely ground*

1 1/2 teaspoons brandy

Raspberry syrup for garnish

1. Place the egg yolks in a microwave-safe bowl. Pierce each one with a toothpick. Cover with plastic wrap and microwave the egg yolks on high for 1 1/2 to 2 minutes, until it reaches the consistency of a soft-boiled egg.

2. In the large bowl of an electric mixer, beat the egg yolks and brown sugar until very thick, about 10 minutes. Turn the mixer to low speed and add 1 cup of the whipped cream. Remove the bowl. Using a wire whisk, fold in the remaining whipped cream, then fold in the pecans, cookie crumbs, and brandy.

3. Pour this mixture into a lightly greased 8-inch springform pan. Cover the surface of the mixture with plastic wrap. This keeps any air from getting in. Cover the entire pan with aluminum foil and place in the freezer.

4. Unmold the torte 1 hour before serving. Wrap a warm cloth around the outside of the mold. Dip a thin spatula in hot water and run it around the outside edge of the torte. Release the spring and remove the ring. Slice the torte using a knife that has been dipped in hot water. Pour a little raspberry syrup over each slice.

*Note: This dessert can stay in the freezer for up to
    1 month. You may wish to use one of the
    other cookie varieties or substitute crushed
    macaroons for the amaretto nut cookies.*

PASSOVER JELLY ROLL

MAKES 8 SERVINGS

Although this is an old fashioned dessert, it's easy to prepare and is delicious made with Passover preserves.

4 large eggs, separated

3/4 cup sugar

1 teaspoon vanilla extract, or 1 packet vanilla sugar

1/4 cup potato starch

1/2 cup matzo cake meal

1 teaspoon baking powder

1/2 teaspoon salt

Confectioners' sugar for dusting

1 cup red raspberry preserves

1. Preheat the oven to 375°F. Thoroughly grease a jelly roll pan approximately 10×15 inches. Cut a piece of parchment or waxed paper about an inch larger on all sides than the baking pan and thoroughly grease one side. Press the paper, greased side up, into the baking pan, allowing the excess to hang over the edges of the pan.

2. In the large bowl of an electric mixer, beat the egg yolks until light and fluffy. Gradually add the sugar and beat until creamy. Add the vanilla and blend in well.

3. Into a medium bowl, sift the potato starch, matzo cake meal, baking powder, and salt together. Add to the egg yolk mixture and beat until well blended and smooth.

4. In a large bowl, beat the egg whites until stiff but not dry. Gently fold the egg whites into the batter.

5. Pour the batter into the prepared pan and spread with a spatula to distribute it evenly. Bake in the center of the oven for 12 minutes.

6. Remove from the oven and immediately loosen the edges of the cake with a small spatula. Turn out onto aluminum foil or a clean dish towel that has been sprinkled generously with confectioners' sugar. Remove the parchment paper (see Note).

7. Spread the cake evenly with preserves. Roll up gently from a long edge. Dust with confectioners' sugar. Let cool completely. To serve, cut into slices approximately 1 inch thick, and top with whipped cream if desired.

Note: You may wish to make the cake roll to this point. Place the cake on aluminum foil or a clean dish towel and roll up, wrapping it in the foil or towel as you go. Refrigerate until ready to spread the preserves.

Variation

Proceed as in above Note. You can also fill the roll with whipped cream, ice cream, or a custard filling.

LEMON THINS

MAKES 4 TO 5 DOZEN

This is the perfect Passover cookie. As a cookie lover, I never seem to get enough of them. The secret to a perfect lemon thin is using no more than a small teaspoon of the dough and not placing them too close together on the baking sheet.

1 large egg

1/3 cup sugar

1 cup potato starch

2 teaspoons grated lemon zest

1 tablespoon freshly squeezed lemon juice

1/2 teaspoon vanilla extract

1/8 teaspoon salt

3 tablespoons vegetable oil

TOPPING

1 tablespoon sugar mixed with 1 teaspoon cinnamon

1. Preheat the oven to 350°F. Lightly grease or spray a baking sheet.

2. Place the egg and sugar in a large bowl and beat with an electric mixer for 3 minutes at high speed. Add the potato starch, lemon zest, lemon juice, vanilla, salt, and oil. Beat on low speed until well blended.

3. Drop small teaspoons of the dough onto the prepared baking sheet, spacing the cookies about 2 inches apart. Bake for 7 to 10 minutes or until the edges are golden brown. Remove the cookies from the oven and sprinkle the tops with the cinnamon sugar. Immediately move all of the cookies to a wire rack to cool. Store in an airtight container.

ROCKY ROAD CANDY

MAKES ABOUT 1¹/₄ POUNDS

This is a favorite with adults and children.

1 cup finely chopped toasted pecans,
  walnuts, almonds, or hazelnuts
  (see Brown Sugar Meringue Crisps,
  page 91, to toast pecans)
2 cups miniature marshmallows
1 cup dark raisins
¹/₂ cup dried cherries or apricots
Two 12-ounce packages semisweet
  chocolate chips

1. Line an 8-inch square baking pan with aluminum foil. In a large bowl, mix the nuts, marshmallows, raisins, and dried cherries or apricots together.

2. Place the chocolate chips in a 4-cup microwave-safe container. Microwave on high for 2 minutes; stir. Microwave 2 minutes more, remove, and stir the chocolate chips until completely melted. Or melt the chocolate chips in a double boiler over very low heat, stirring constantly.

3. Spread half of the melted chocolate evenly on top of the foil in the pan. Distribute the marshmallow mixture over the melted chocolate. Spread the remaining melted chocolate on top. Place in the refrigerator to harden. Remove and break into bite-size pieces.

Variation: Chocolate Clusters
Stir the marshmallow mixture into the melted chocolate. Drop by teaspoons onto a foil-lined jelly roll pan and refrigerate for several hours until hard.

WATERMELON ICE

MAKES ABOUT 1 QUART

A perfect make-ahead spring or summer dessert.

6 cups watermelon chunks, seeded

3 tablespoons freshly squeezed lemon juice

*1 teaspoon rose flavoring (see Note)
   or red raspberry syrup*

1 cup sugar

2 envelopes unflavored gelatin

1 cup boiling water

1. Puree the watermelon with the lemon juice in a food processor or blender.

2. Into a large bowl, force the puree through a fine sieve or food mill to remove any fiber, then stir in the rose flavoring.

3. In a medium bowl, whisk together the sugar and gelatin. Slowly add the boiling water and stir to dissolve the sugar. Add to the pureed melon and mix well. Pour the mixture into a shallow metal bowl or cake pan and freeze until solid, about 6 hours or overnight.

4. Break the frozen watermelon into chunks and process or blend in small batches until smooth. Serve immediately. Should you have any left over, return it to the food processor or blender. Add a little heavy cream, process until smooth, and re-freeze. You'll have sorbet.

Note: Rose flavoring is used in many Sephardic recipes. It can be found in a bakery supply shop or Indian food store. Use a new, unopened bottle for Passover.

THE FOURTH CUP

KOSHER WINES, SPIRITS, AND LIQUEURS FOR PASSOVER

WHAT MAKES WINE KOSHER FOR PASSOVER?

1. Kosher wine must be produced and supervised exclusively by an orthodox, Sabbath-observant, kosher supervisor who is knowledgeable in the kosher laws involved in winemaking. The injunction against someone who is not Jewish touching the wine originated in biblical times, when wine was used by some for idol worship.

2. Jewish dietary laws prevent the use of any leavened grain or animal-based ingredients in the winemaking process. If the wine is kosher for Passover, you will find a "P" on the label of the bottle.

3. All winemaking equipment that comes into contact with the grape juice and/or wine must be cleansed with nonchemical, vegetable-based cleansers and must not be used for the production of nonkosher wines.

4. No winemaking is allowed to be done on Friday nights, on the Sabbath, or on any of the Jewish holidays.

5. Today many kosher wines are "mevusahl wines," or flash-heated/pasteurized. These are kosher even if handled by non-Jewish personnel. Most Orthodox caterers prefer to use these wines at large functions because many of their employees are not Jewish.

6. Any grape from any region or nation may be used to produce a kosher wine.

PASSOVER WINES, LIQUEURS, AND BRANDIES

No longer are the sweet and heavy kosher Malaga wines the only choice to accompany the Passover Seder's symbolic foods and the festive meal or to be used for the required four cups of wine. Today the kosher wine industry provides a selection that far surpasses our wildest dreams. Although a variety of kosher Passover wines are suggested with the Seder menus in chapter IV, the following recommended list is more inclusive.

RED WINES

New York

Kesser Seven Seventy: Sweet kiddush wine.

Kedem Concord Grape: Fruity and hearty, extra heavy.

Kedem Cream Concord: Medium sweet, low in alcohol, smooth.

France

Herzog Selections De La Grave: Dry, complex, well-balanced Bordeaux. Serve with heavy main courses of meat.

Herzog Selections Merlot Vin de Pays: Soft, full, and aromatic, with a supple allure. Serve with light courses of chicken or meat.

Baron Rothschild Haut Medoc: Delicate Bordeaux of complexity and classic style. World class. Serve with heavy, sauced meats or charcoal-broiled steaks.

Israel/The Golan Heights

Golan Cabernet Sauvignon: A king of a Cabernet, rich and flavorful, with a fine balance and finish. Enjoy with a rich main entrée.

Yarden Merlot: In the past this was voted best wine in the world at the Vinexpo in France. It fills your mouth with abundant flavor and a long, lingering finish. Serve with lighter sauced, medium-flavored meat.

California

Baron Herzog Cabernet Sauvignon: A full, rich wine of unmistakable elegance and depth. Serve with charcoal-broiled steaks and rich main dishes.

Hagafen 1989 Cabernet Sauvignon Reserve: Black with deep purple rim. Moderately full-bodied. Balanced acidity. Highly extracted and oaked. Flavors of leather, black fruits, and violets. In the mouth, ripe, juicy fruit is framed by wood and tannins. Subtle finish. Enjoy with brisket, roast turkey, or goose.

Hagafen 1993 Cabernet Sauvignon: Classic Napa Valley Cabernet Sauvignon, fruity with oak aromas, soft, round, and balanced. Enjoy with red meats and roasted poultry.

Weinstock Pinot Noir: Dry, fruity, with a fresh finish. Serve with lightly sauced, medium-flavored meats and turkey.

Weinstock 1994 Napa Gamay: A fresh light red wine that bursts with raspberry and strawberry flavor. Goes with fish, fowl, or meat.

SPARKLING WINES

Hagafen 1993 Chardonnay Reserve: (This was served at a White House dinner in 1996, when the late Prime Minister Yitzak Rabin visited.)

WHITE WINES

Israel/The Golan Heights

Yarden Sauvignon Blanc: Crisp, bright, and fresh. Israel's best. Enjoy with fish and fruity main courses.

Yarden Chardonnay: Very rich, like a great white French Burgundy. Lots of oak and complexity. Serve with rich fish such as salmon.

Yarden Port Blanc: Sweet dessert wine with complexity and a firm acidity that makes it taste fresh and lively, with a wonderful aroma.

California

Baron Herzog Chardonnay: An outstanding white wine with full body, noble character, and distinctive flavor. Serve with fish and fruity main courses.

Herzog Late Harvest Johannisberg Riesling: Sweet, ripe, and concentrated, subtly scented with luscious flavor. Great for dessert.

Hagafen 1993 Chardonnay Reserve: Spicy and creamy flavors of melted butter, vanilla, and butterscotch. Great for holiday dining. (This was served at the White House with grilled salmon.)

Hagafen 1995 Chardonnay:
Lovely white wine, green apple–pear bouquet. This wine goes well with curried, chicken, vegetarian, and fish dishes.

Weinstock White Zinfandel:
"Best of California" Gold 1995. This light pink wine exhibits cranberry and raspberry aromas. This light wine can be served with appetizers before dinner.

Barentura Asti Spumante (Italy):
A semisweet sparking wine of exceptional taste.

Spirits, Liqueur, Brandy

Should some of these selections be unavailable in your area, contact a local wine retailer and ask them to place a special order with their distributor. You may need to pay a premium, and you will need to plan ahead. Due to state regulations, some of these selections may be unavailable in your area. Spirits, liqueurs, and brandy that are kosher for Passover will have a "P" on the label of the bottle.

Spirits

Jamaica
Kedem Vodka

Liqueurs

Italy
Bartenura: Hazelnut, amaretto, and sambuca liqueurs

Israel
Hallelujah: Orange brandy/liqueur

Sabra: Orange liqueur, chocolated flavored

Cognac and Brandy

Israel
Askalon Arack Extra Fine

Alouf Arack 100 proof

France
Montalgne Cognac VSOP

Cognac "Les Trols Etolles"

Boukha Bokobsa fig brandy

The Hagafen red and white wines are recommended by Ernie Weir, winemaker and owner of Hagafen Cellars, Napa, California. All other wines, spirits, liqueurs, and brandies are recommended by Jay Buchsbaum, Vice President Marketing, Royal Kedem Wine Corporation, Brooklyn, New York.

APPENDICES

INGREDIENT SUBSTITUTIONS FOR PASSOVER

This list of food substitutions will enable you to convert many of your favorite recipes to *kosher l'Pesach* (kosher for Passover).

Ingredients	*Substitute*
3/4 cup bread crumbs	One 12-ounce box soup nuts (*mandlen*), ground.
1 ounce chocolate	3 tablespoons cocoa plus 1 tablespoon shortening or use a Passover chocolate bar
cornstarch	potato starch
1 cup confectioners' sugar	1 cup minus 1/2 tablespoon granulated sugar, pulverized in a blender and sifted together with 1 1/2 teaspoons potato starch
1 cup all-purpose flour for baking	5/8 cup (3/4 cup minus 2 tablespoons) matzo cake meal or potato starch, or a combination sifted together
1 tablespoon flour as a sauce thickener	1/2 tablespoon potato starch or 1 egg yolk
1 cup of matzo meal	Three matzos or 2 cups matzo farfel processed 45 seconds to 1 minute
gelatin	Kosher for Passover gelatin

GLOSSARY

AFIKOMAN (OFF-ee-comb-man):

"Dessert." The middle matzo: the last ceremonial food eaten at a Seder.

ASHKENAZIC (Osh-keh-NOZ-zeek):

Refers to Jewish people who migrated from central and eastern European countries.

BAYTZAH (BAYTZ-ah):

A roasted egg placed on the Seder plate symbolizing the festival offering brought to the temple.

BRIS (BRISS):

"Covenant." Refers to the circumcision ceremony.

CHAG HA-MATZOT (HA-gah MA-tsot):

The Feast of Unleavened Bread, Passover.

CHAG HA-PESACH (HA-gah PAY-sahk):

The pesach, or "paschal" offering, of a lamb or calf.

CHAROSET (HA-row-SET):

A mixture of chopped fruit, nuts, and wine used on the Seder plate to symbolize the mortar used in Egypt by Jewish slaves building Pharoah's stone cities of Pithom and Raames.

CHOMETZ (HAW-METZ):

Leavened or fermented food; foods not eaten during Passover.

ELIJAH:

A prophet said to visit each Passover Seder to herald freedom and redemption. A goblet filled with wine is placed on the Seder table to welcome Elijah.

FLEISHIG (FLAY-sheeg):

Word used for meat, poultry, and food products prepared with animal fat. Not to be eaten with dairy.

GEFILTE FISH (ge-FILL-teh fish):

Fish balls or cakes made of various chopped or ground fish and seasonings, then cooked in fish stock. For observant Jews, work is not allowed on the Sabbath. Eating a fish with the bones intact is considered work!

GRIBENES (GRIB-ends):

Chicken or goose skin rendered with its fat when preparing schmaltz.

HAGGADAH (HA-GOD-dah):

The book used at the Passover Seder, which tells the story of Exodus. The Haggadah also explains the Passover symbols and contains liturgical text, prayers, and songs.

HILLEL (HILL-el):

A great scholar and teacher who lived in the third century C.E.

HILLEL'S SANDWICH:

Symbolic sandwich. In observance of the precept "They shall eat [the paschal lamb] together with matzo and bitter herbs," the Jewish scholar Hillel combined the bitter herbs and charoset on matzo and ate them together.

KAARAH (CAR-AH):

The Seder plate, which contains representative portions of the ceremonial foods, each one having a symbolic meaning.

KARPAS (CAR-PASS):

Parsley or celery placed on the Seder plate, symbolizing springtime, hope, and renewal.

KIDDUSH (KI-DISH):

Hebrew for "sanctification." A prayer and ceremony that is used on the Sabbath and Jewish holy days. This prayer is said over the wine poured into a kiddush cup.

KIDDUSH CUP:

Cup used by the leader blessing the wine at the Seder meal, beginning of the Sabbath, or other holy day.

KOHEN (KO-HAYN):

The head priest. Aaron, the brother of Moses, was the first high priest, of all Hebrew priests, who conducted services in the great temple in Jerusalem.

KOSHER (KO-SHER):

"Fitting." Dietary laws that govern Jewish foods, monitored under "strict orthodox supervision" by a rabbi or rabbinical student knowledgeable in the kosher laws.

KOSHER L'PESACH (KO-SHER L'PAY-SAHK):

Kosher for Passover. Foods permitted to be eaten during Passover are said to be kosher l'Pesach.

LEVI (LEE-VIE):

Assistant to the priests in the temple.

LEVIVOT (LEH-VI-VOTE):

Fritters made with vegetables or cheese.

MALAGA (MAH-LAHG-A):

Sweet, heavy kosher wine used on Sabbath and holidays.

MANDLEN (MAHND-LEN):

Miniature puff pastry balls added to soup.

MAROR (MAR-OR):

A bitter herb placed on the Seder plate, symbolizing the bitterness of the slavery experienced by Jews in Egypt.

MATZO (MOTT-SEH),
PLURAL MATZOS (MOTT-SEZ):

Bread baked without leavening.

MILCHIG (MILK-HEEG):

Food that contains milk or milk products. Not eaten with meat or any products containing animal fat.

NISAN (KNEE-SUN):

The first month in the Hebrew calendar. Passover and the first Seder begin at sundown the fourteenth day of this month.

NOSH (RHYMES WITH GOSH):

Snack.

PAREVE (PA-REV) OR PARVE (PAR-VA):

Words used on food products to indicate that they contain neither meat nor milk. These products are neutral and may be eaten with milk or meat.

PESACH (PAY-SAHK):

Passover in Hebrew.

SCHMALTZ (SHMOLL-TS):

Rendered chicken or goose fat.

SEDER (SAY-DER):

"Order of the ritual." Seder begins at sundown, the evening before the first day of the Passover holiday.

SEPHARDIC (SEH-FAR-DEEK):

Refers to Jewish people who migrated from Mediterranean countries.

SHOCHET (SHOW-KHET):

An authorized slaughterer of meat and fowl, according to kosher laws.

TAM (TOM):

Flavor.

TORAH (TORE-AH):

Jewish scripture (The Five Books of Moses) and other oral and written teachings.

TZIMMES (TSIM-MESS):

"To the eating." A side dish of mixed cooked vegetables and fruits, slightly sweetened.

YARMULKAH (YAHR-M'L-KEH):

Head covering worn by those following traditional Jewish law. Kippah (KEE-pa) in Hebrew.

ZEROAH (ZAIR-OH-AH):

A roasted lamb shank bone or chicken wing placed on the Seder plate, representing the ancient sacrifice of the Paschal lamb.

FUTURE DATES OF PASSOVER

Passover on the Hebrew calendar always begins at sundown on the evening of the fourteenth day of Nisan, which is when the first Seder is held. This corresponds to the month of March or April on the secular calendar.

MAIL-ORDER GIFT CATALOGS

Invited for a Seder at someone else's home and need just the right item to bring the hostess? Need to send a holiday gift package to friends or family at home or in Israel? These Jewish catalogs can come to the rescue.

Galerie Robin
To order a catalog, call 1-800-635-8279, or fax (513) 563-8026

Judaica Occasions
To order a catalog, call 1-800-336-2291, or fax (914) 356-8502

The Source for Everything Jewish
To order a catalog, call 1-800-552-4088, or fax (847) 966-4033

GOURMET KOSHER FOOD CATALOGS

For gourmet Passover food items, I've had great results with these two mail-order catalogs, especially when I needed to send holiday gift packages to my friends and family in Israel.

Kosher Cornucopia
To order a catalog, call 1-800-756-7437, or fax (914) 482-3643

The Kosher Connection
To order a catalog, call 1-800-950-7227, or fax 503-297-0417

BIBLIOGRAPHY

Encyclopaedia Judaica Jerusalem, Vols. 8, 10, 11, 13. Jerusalem, Israel: Keter Publishing House Ltd., 1971.

Friedland, Susan R. *The Passover Table.* New York: HarperCollins Publishers, Inc., 1994.

Gaster, Theodor H. *Festivals of the Jewish Year.* New York: Morrow Quill Paperbacks, 1978.

Goodman, Hanna. *Jewish Cooking Around the World.* Philadelphia: The Jewish Publication Society of America, 1973.

Marks, Copeland. *Sephardic Cooking.* New York: Donald I. Fine, Inc., Primus, 1992.

Moryoussef, Viviane and Nina. *Moroccan Jewish Cookery.* Translated by Shirley Kay. Paris, France: SEFA International, and Casablanca, Morocco: Sochepress, 1983.

Nathan, Joan. *Jewish Cooking in America.* New York: Alfred A. Knopf, 1994.

Rosten, Leo. *The Joys of Yiddish.* New York, Toronto, London, Sydney: McGraw-Hill Book Company, 1968.

Shosteck, Patti. *A Lexicon of Jewish Cooking.* Chicago: Contemporary Books, Inc., 1979.

Stavroulakis, Nicholas. *Cookbook of the Jews of Greece.* Port Jefferson, New York: Cadmus Press, 1986.

Wolfson, Ron, *The Passover Seder.* Woodstock, Vermont: Jewish Lights Publishing, 1996.

INDEX

AGGADAHS?   I'M JEWISH, BUT I'VE NEVER COOKED WITH MATZO.   MY HU
ALLY HAVE TO DRINK FOUR GLASSES OF WINE?   WHEN IS THIS SERVICE GO
O ! IT'S MY TURN TO MAKE THE PASSOVER SEDER!   MY MOTHER IS COMIN-
- BE KOSHER?   WHO SELLS HAGGADAHS?   I'M JEWISH, BUT I'VE NEVER CO
THE CEREMONY?   DO YOU REALLY HAVE TO DRINK FOUR GLASSES OF W
GIN?   WHERE DO I BEGIN?   OH NO ! IT'S MY TURN TO MAKE THE PASSOV
EP KOSHER. DOES A SEDER HAVE TO BE KOSHER?   WHO SELLS HAGGADAH
WISH—HOW CAN HE PARTICIPATE IN THE CEREMONY?   DO YOU REALLY
ER?   WHEN DOES THE REAL MEAL BEGIN?   WHERE DO I BEGIN?   OH NO
IS MY MOTHER-IN-LAW!   I DON'T KEEP KOSHER. DOES A SEDER HAVE TO
TH MATZO.   MY HUSBAND'S NOT JEWISH—HOW CAN HE PARTICIPATE IN
HEN IS THIS SERVICE GONNA BE OVER?   WHEN DOES THE REAL MEAL BEGIN
Y MOTHER IS COMING AND SO IS MY MOTHER-IN-LAW!   I DON'T KEEP K
WISH, BUT I'VE NEVER COOKED WITH MATZO.   MY HUSBAND'S NOT JEWI
RINK FOUR GLASSES OF WINE?   WHEN IS THIS SERVICE GONNA BE OVER?
RN TO MAKE THE PASSOVER SEDER!   MY MOTHER IS COMING AND SO IS M
HO SELLS HAGGADAHS?   I'M JEWISH, BUT I'VE NEVER COOKED WITH MAT
?   DO YOU REALLY HAVE TO DRINK FOUR GLASSES OF WINE?   WHEN IS
I BEGIN?   OH NO ! IT'S MY TURN TO MAKE THE PASSOVER SEDER!   MY
ES A SEDER HAVE TO BE KOSHER?   WHO SELLS HAGGADAHS?   I'M JEWIS
N HE PARTICIPATE IN THE CEREMONY?   DO YOU REALLY HAVE TO DRIN
ES THE REAL MEAL BEGIN?   WHERE DO I BEGIN?   OH NO ! IT'S MY TURN
-IN-LAW!   I DON'T KEEP KOSHER. DOES A SEDER HAVE TO BE KOSHER?
Y HUSBAND'S NOT JEWISH—HOW CAN HE PARTICIPATE IN THE CEREMONY?
CE GONNA BE OVER?   WHEN DOES THE REAL MEAL BEGIN?   WHERE DO I
COMING AND SO IS MY MOTHER-IN-LAW!   I DON'T KEEP KOSHER. DOES A
VER COOKED WITH MATZO.   MY HUSBAND'S NOT JEWISH—HOW CAN HE P
OF WINE?   WHEN IS THIS SERVICE GONNA BE OVER?   WHEN DOES THE M
SSOVER SEDER!   MY MOTHER IS COMING AND SO IS MY MOTHER-IN-LA'
GGADAHS?   I'M JEWISH, BUT I'VE NEVER COOKED WITH MATZO.   MY HU
ALLY HAVE TO DRINK FOUR GLASSES OF WINE?   WHEN IS THIS SERVICE GO
! IT'S MY TURN TO MAKE THE PASSOVER SEDER!   MY MOTHER IS COMIN
BE KOSHER?   WHO SELLS HAGGADAHS?   I'M JEWISH, BUT I'VE NEVER CO
THE CEREMONY?   DO YOU REALLY HAVE TO DRINK FOUR GLASSES OF W